STU ... IN ... ... No. 19

General Editor

David Da...

Already

Already published in the series (*continued*):

E. M. FORSTER:
A PASSAGE TO INDIA

by

JOHN COLMER

Professor of English
The University of Adelaide

EDWARD ARNOLD

First published 1967 by
Edward Arnold (Publishers) Ltd
41 Bedford Square, London WC1B 3DQ

Reprinted 1969, 1974, 1976, 1978, 1980, 1982

ISBN: 0 7131 5111 0

*Printed and bound in Great Britain at
The Camelot Press Ltd, Southampton*

General Preface

The object of this series is to provide studies of individual novels, plays and groups of poems and essays which are known to be widely read by students. The emphasis is on clarification and evaluation; biographical and historical facts, while they may be discussed when they throw light on particular elements in a writer's work, are generally subordinated to critical discussion. What kind of work is this? What exactly goes on here? How good is this work, and why? These are the questions that each writer will try to answer.

It should be emphasized that these studies are written on the assumption that the reader has already read carefully the work discussed. The objective is not to enable students to deliver opinions about works they have not read, nor is it to provide ready-made ideas to be applied to works that have been read. In one sense all critical interpretation can be regarded as foisting opinions on readers, but to accept this is to deny the advantages of any sort of critical discussion directed at students or indeed at anybody else. The aim of these studies is to provide what Coleridge called in another context 'aids to reflection' about the works discussed. The interpretations are offered as suggestive rather than as definitive, in the hope of stimulating the reader into developing further his own insights. This is after all the function of all critical discourse among sensible people.

Because of the interest which this kind of study has aroused, it has been decided to extend it first from merely English literature to include also some selected works of American literature and now further to include selected works in English by Commonwealth writers. The criterion will remain that the book studied is important in itself and is widely read by students.

DAVID DAICHES

Acknowledgements

I am grateful to E. M. Forster for giving his personal blessing to this study and I hope he will think the pages justify his faith. To all previous critics of Forster's novels I owe a great but indefinable debt.

In dealing with crucial episodes I have enjoyed the privilege of consulting Robert L. Harrison's study of the manuscripts of *A Passage to India*, an unpublished Ph.D. thesis presented at the University of Texas. I am grateful to the University of Texas Library for providing me with photo copies and for answering queries about manuscripts.

Professor H. J. Oliver, who has already contributed to our understanding of this novel, and Mr. S. C. Harrex, who has made a special study of the Indian novel in English, both kindly agreed to read an early draft. I am grateful to them and to Mr. Manfred Mackenzie for many valuable suggestions and to my wife for her sensitive insight into Forster's art.

Contents

By far the most valuable things, which we know or can imagine, are certain states of consciousness, which may be roughly described as the pleasures of human intercourse and the enjoyment of beautiful objects . . . it is only for the sake of these things—in order that as much of them as possible may at some time exist—that anyone can be justified in performing any public or private duty; . . . it is they . . . that form the rational ultimate end of human action and the sole criterion of social progress. . . .

G. E. Moore, *Principia Ethica*

Only connect the prose and the passion, and both will be exalted, and human love will be seen at its height.

E. M. Forster, *Howards End*

Music, though it does not employ human beings, though it is governed by intricate laws, nevertheless does offer in its final expression a type of beauty which fiction might achieve in its own way. Expansion. That is the idea the novelist must cling to. Not completion. Not rounding off but opening out.

E. M. Forster, *Aspects of the Novel*

1. *What kind of novel is it?*

E. M. Forster's *A Passage to India* is a novel that explores the difficulties men face in trying to understand each other and the universe; it is not primarily concerned with questions of rule and race, although it has often been suggested that it is. Here, as in his other novels, Forster concentrates on the life of the individual and ignores the claims of society, adopting the position defined by Philip Herriton in the early novel *Where Angels Fear to Tread*: 'Society *is* invincible—to a certain degree. But your real life is your own, and nothing can touch it.' In *A Passage to India* racial prejudice, religious differences, climate, snobbery, problems of communication all touch the 'real life' of the individual, but politics hardly at all. Nevertheless, in the years that led up to the partition of India and Pakistan and brought about independence for many African and Asian countries, the novel has often been read for its topical relevance. To say that it is not a novel about political problems may diminish its appeal to many Indian, African and Asian readers, for whom politics seem of paramount importance, but it need not do so if they recognise that in exploring the ultimate mystery of life Forster assigns a subordinate role to all merely human relations, not only to political ones, seeing man's attempts to create unity dominated and diminished by forces he cannot control.

The 'passage' that Forster explores is not simply the path to greater understanding of India, but man's quest for ultimate truth. The title of the novel is drawn from Walt Whitman's poem 'Passage to India', as Forster himself has acknowledged. Just as the poem stresses the need to combine the successes of Western civilisation with a new exploration of spiritual experiences as wonderful as the opening of the Suez Canal or the building of the American railways, so Forster's novel relates the ideas of human harmony to the secrets of the inner life and the mystery of the whole universe.

> Passage to more than India!
> O secret of the earth and sky!
> . . . .
> Sail forth—steer for the deep water only,

> Reckless O Soul, exploring, I with thee, and thou with me,
> For we are bound where mariner has not yet dared to go,
> And we will risk the ship, ourselves and all.

However dissimilar the voices of the ironic English novelist and the romantic American poet may appear, they speak of a similar quest.

India, which Forster first visited in 1912–13 and to which he returned as the acting Private Secretary of the Rajah of Dewas Senior in 1921, offered a vast physical and mental landscape in which to develop more fully many of the themes he had already explored in novels and short stories. These may be conveniently summarised as the importance of personal relations, the sanctity of the emotional life, the problems of reconciling worldly success and spiritual salvation, the importance of the relationship of man and nature. Already in the Italian novels, *A Room with a View* (1908) and *Where Angels Fear to Tread* (1905), he had traced the effects on personal relations of differences in race, culture and national temperament. But the contrasts in these early novels between English and Italian values are less complex than those between English, Muslim and Hindu in *A Passage to India*. There is a clear-cut distinction between the instinctive passionate life of Italy and the conventional, snob-ridden world of suburban England ('Sawston'). In *A Passage to India* there is no such sharp division and the range is altogether wider, extending from the ruling British and wealthy Indians to 'humanity grading and drifting beyond the educated vision, until no earthly invitation can embrace it'. Contrast is no longer a device for measuring antithetical ways of life, but serves as an index of the mystery—or muddle—that lies at the heart of the universe. Then again the natural world is now no longer a source of ultimate good as it was for Forster's earlier characters, Stephen in *The Longest Journey* (1907), George Emerson in *A Room with a View*, or Gino in *Where Angels Fear to Tread*, but is alien, hostile, full of menace. From the first shifting perspectives of Chandrapore to the final description of Fielding and Aziz's last ride together, the Indian landscape dominates the novel, dwarfing the protagonists, challenging the established values of Western civilisation, a civilisation that has been built on the idea that it is possible to achieve a 'harmony between the works of man and the earth that holds them, the civilisation that has escaped muddle, the spirit in a reasonable form, with flesh and blood subsisting'. As G. Lowes Dickinson, Forster's close friend and travelling companion in 1912, had pointed out in his *Greek View of*

Life (a book that Forster knew and admired), everything in the modern world challenges this idea of harmony. India provided Forster with an 'objective correlative' for the forces against which all humanistic endeavour is pitted. He retains a severely qualified faith in this endeavour, but does not perhaps provide sufficient grounds for doing so. Depending on where we place the stress and how sensitive we are to the tensions between poetic vision and ironic comment, the novel may appear to offer a nihilistic reading of life, or a humanistic one, or a comprehensive vision which allows for both extremes—and for much else besides—and whose chief appeal lies in its enigmatic detachment and perfection of artistic design.

Three of the novelist's own phrases provide us with the keys to Forster's meaning and method in *A Passage to India*. These are: 'personal relations', 'only connect', and 'expansion . . . not completion'. The first defines the main theme of all his novels, the second, which he uses in *Howards End*, epitomises his ideal of achieving a harmony between the discordant elements within man himself and between man and the universe, the third points to his exploitation of musical form and warns us against attempting to define and limit the meaning of the novel. In *Aspects of the Novel*, the lectures Forster delivered at Cambridge three years after the publication of *A Passage to India*, he drew frequent analogies between fictional and musical composition in discussing 'Pattern and Rhythm'. 'When the symphony is over, we feel that the notes and tunes comprising it have been liberated, they have found in the rhythm of the whole their individual freedom. Cannot the novel be like that?' In his last novel he supplies his own answer. It can. Our first task then is to tune our ears to the novelist's notes, to recognise the announcement of his major themes in the opening chapters of the three main sections, and to appreciate the function of his large-scale tripartite musical form: Mosque, Caves, Temple. As in any great work of art, form and meaning are organically related. The possibility that only an echoing void lies at the heart of the universe and the vision of a harmony that transcends the limitations of human achievement are reconciled through the novel's symphonic form.

2. Mosque

(i) India. Caves, city, civil station, sky

The opening chapter does much more than introduce us to the Indian city of Chandrapore. It establishes a series of striking contrasts: between the cool discriminating mind of the author and the hot undifferentiated mass of his material—India; between the disordered, mean life of the city of Chandrapore and the rationally ordered but sterile life of the English civil station; between the images of earthly disharmony and the image of the 'overarching sky'. The sky is an ambiguous but richly evocative image that frequently recurs and which, according to context, suggests the possibility of harmony (as in its first use in Chapter I), or power, or beauty, or infinity. The last recurrence of the image in the final words of the novel seems to express Forster's belief that human harmony is not always and everywhere unattainable. Although all India inhibits perfect friendship between Fielding and Aziz and speaking through its hundred voices says ' "No, not yet" ', the sky nevertheless says ' "No, not there".' As so often in this novel the promise of harmony recedes the very moment it is given expression. The infinite offers a promise denied by the finite world of man's everyday experience but the promise is not wholly real and satisfying, because Forster inhabits and creates a relativistic world in which there is no place for God or any divine principle that might fully validate this vision of potential harmony.

In a fictional world, in which there are no absolutes but only relative values, perspective, or point of view, must assume a special importance. Forster's control of perspective enables him to create a lively sense of the immense diversity of life and also to make us feel that since each human being sees the world through different eyes, full communication becomes difficult if not impossible. Family relationships, love, friendship, political understanding are all affected. In the first chapter perspective is used in Forster's description of landscape to ease us into the unfamiliar Indian world in the most natural way, and to suggest that human life is dominated by non-human forces, by the earth and sky.

The informality of style in the opening paragraph is deceptive. The casual opening, 'Except in the Marabar Caves' is an example of the art that hides art; in fact, it is part of an intensely imagined and organised whole, the Caves returning again and again like a musical leitmotiv, gathering ominous overtones with each repetition. The intimate, relaxed, almost conversational tone immediately establishes an easy relationship between writer and reader. The author's character as an ironic, detached, precise observer quickly emerges through the long sequence of qualifying phrases ('edged rather than washed', 'as the Ganges happens not to be holy there'), so too does the character of the amorphous landscape. Negative verbs and adjectives strip life of all beauty and significance. The first unqualified and rhythmically stressed verbs speak of destruction, death, and putrefaction. 'Houses do fall, people are drowned and left rotting.' The rhythmic repetitions, 'swelling here, shrinking there' reinforce the effect of the simile that compares the Indians to 'some low but indestructible form of life'. This picture of life implicitly challenges our common assumptions about man's power to dominate nature.

The opening sentence of the next paragraph ('Inland, the prospect alters') prepares us for the changes of view and human attitude that spring from a different perspective. From the vantage point of the second rise in ground on which the English civil station is built, 'Chandrapore appears to be a totally different place. It is a city of gardens. It is no city, but a forest sparsely scattered with huts. It is a tropical pleasaunce washed by a noble river.' The phrasing here clearly suggests the illusory nature of the vision, but the description of the trees that are nourished by ancient water tanks (or artificial lakes), that have 'more strength than man or his works', and which 'build a city for the birds', offers a momentary vision of an area of beauty midway between the squalor of Chandrapore and the sterility of the civil station. But the trees 'screen' Chandrapore from British eyes. Newcomers have to be driven down to see the real squalor to 'acquire disillusionment'. The writing is complex here. Slight modulations of tone suggest subtle changes in perspective and emotional response. What is indisputable is that Forster links the British angle of vision with illusion, but dissociates it from appreciation of real beauty. In rather prim, mannered Biblical phrases he emphasises the aesthetic neutrality of the English civil station: 'It charms not, neither does it repel.' Later this respectable ordered mediocrity is linked in our minds with other characteristics of the ruling

British: Ronny's sterile brand of public school religion, the unthinking acceptance of a code of behaviour, the idea that interest in art is bad form, the use of the word 'pukka' as an infallible standard. The limitations of the ruling British emerge from the faintly ironic account of the 'sensibly planned' features of the station with its roads that 'intersect at right angles'. The achievements of a loveless, unimaginative rationalism are apparently as insignificant as those of 'abased' humanity in Chandrapore. The English civil station 'has nothing hideous in it, and only the view is beautiful; it shares nothing with the city except the overarching sky'.

In this first occurrence of the key image of the overarching sky we feel something of a tension between the negative context in which it is introduced and the positive promise of a transcendent harmony that it appears to offer. The two concluding paragraphs of the chapter develop contrasting aspects of the sky—its remote beauty and its direct influence on the earth. On the one hand it suggests permanence within a process of change, a rounded perfection of beauty, with the night sky conveying hints of infinity; on the other hand it is shown as all-powerful, settling everything—'not only climates and seasons but when the earth shall be beautiful.' Finally, the implied contrast between the two extremes of sky and earth leads to the abrupt, slightly sinister re-introduction of the Marabar hills and caves. The curve of earth that answers the curve of sky is interrupted by 'the fists and fingers' of the hills.

(ii) *Indians. 'Is it possible to be friends with an Englishman?'*

Now that Forster has announced his major themes through the description of the Indian landscape, he bounces us into the middle of a conversation between three Indians. They are Dr. Aziz and the two lawyers, Mahmoud Ali and Hamidullah. Aziz, from the moment that he throws down his bicycle before a servant can catch it, comes instantly to life; he is animated, impulsive, careless, impractical, talkative, delights in sensuous pleasures and is sensitive to beauty. He radiates human warmth. Nothing that he does or says (not even his ignoble suspicions about Fielding's motives in sparing Adela) can erase the first impact of this likeable young Muslim doctor. The subject of the conversation, whether it is possible to be friends with an Englishman, enables Forster to reveal the shifting variety of views held even among the Indians themselves. Mahmoud Ali argued that it was not possible to be

friends, 'Hamidullah disagreed, but with so many reservations tha[
was no friction between them'. Useless to look for any precisely d₵......
attitudes here. Hamidullah, who remembers the friendship he had
enjoyed when he was an undergraduate at Cambridge, argues that it is
possible in England though not in India. Unobtrusively the dialogue
draws attention to the way India changes English people so that they
become unfeeling, proud and autocratic; it also introduces some of the
English characters through the prejudiced eyes of the three Indians. In a
novel that is centrally concerned with human misunderstanding, it is
important that the reader should frequently see one group of characters
through the eyes of another. In this novel he must be prepared to be
responsive to the tones of each speech and to the comments slipped in
by the author; he will then allow for the distortions that spring from
personal bias and racial prejudice, for example he will allow for the
latter in the bitter amusement derived by the Indians from running
down their English masters. Tone is so deftly managed that one is
tempted to think that direct authorial comments such as those on Aziz's
ignorance of Mrs. Turton's character are unnecessary: Forster comments,
'He too generalised from his disappointments—it is difficult for members
of a subject race to do otherwise.' The comment is necessary, however,
since it establishes the novelist's superior knowledge and his charitable
understanding of human limitation and weakness; it also suggests his
firm control over his characters. It is vital for the success of Forster's
novel that the reader's confidence in the author's superior, ironic but
compassionate vision should be created from the beginning.

The writing is so compressed and economical that we are in danger of
missing important details on a first reading. Forster wished to link this
chapter with what follows as closely as possible as a comparison of an
early MS. version with the printed text reveals. Compare '. . . Mrs.
Turton takes bribes, red nose is apparently a bachelor' with '. . . Mrs.
Turton takes bribes, Mrs. Red-nose does not and cannot, because so far
there is no Mrs. Red-nose'. The second version, which is that of the
published text, foreshadows more clearly the theme of Adela's and
Ronny's (Red-nose's) relationship. Further indirect information is
released in the interview between Mrs. Moore and Aziz in the mosque.

The presentation of a single incident through different eyes reveals
how the motives behind human actions are misunderstood as the result
of prejudice and lack of imagination. At first Ronny Heaslop's insulting
behaviour towards one of the Indian lawyers is presented through

Indian eyes to support the argument that young Englishmen deteriorate as soon as they arrive in the country: when he first came to Chandrapore the 'red-nose boy' politely offered a cigarette to an Indian lawyer, now he insults him in court. In the next chapter we see the same two incidents through Ronny's eyes, when he is explaining to his mother how easy it is to make mistakes when one first arrives:

> Soon after I came out I asked one of the pleaders to have a smoke with me—only a cigarette mind. I found afterwards that he had sent touts all over the bazaar to announce the fact—told all the litigants, 'Oh, you'd better come to my Vakil Mahmoud Ali—he's in with the City Magistrate.' Ever since then I've dropped on him in court as hard as I could. It's taught me a lesson, and I hope him.

His mother gently exposes his lack of logic by pointing out that the lesson he should have learnt was to invite all the pleaders, but such simple views have no place in Chandrapore. Such 'double takes' are common in this novel; for example in the two accounts of the collar stud episode and of Aziz's polo playing with the English officer. Their function is to show how passion and prejudice lead people to misjudge each other's characters, actions, and motives. The technique as practised by Forster has the advantage of making the reader feel directly involved in the process of discovering the real truth, while at the same time controlling his actual responses. Only a particularly obtuse reader insensitive to irony would conclude that Ronny had learned the right lesson.

In its inconsistency, impetuous flow, and brittle pettiness, the conversation between the three Indians succeeds very well in suggesting a form of social intercourse very unlike that which exists among the ruling British; the lively stream of words is quite different from the dull stereotyped verbal counters exchanged at the English club. Both sides show a childish pettiness, but the behaviour of the Indians seems more excusable, since it is presented from a sympathetic, compassionate point of view. Moreover, their own good humour and pathos soften the sense of social injustice. Once Aziz has been arrested, however, the Indians' criticism of the British acquires a rancorous tone that is totally absent in this first scene.

The impulsive chatterbox Aziz, a creature of sudden moods, hypersensitive, easily irritated by his aunt's suggestion that he should marry (an irritation that skilfully foreshadows his embarrassment when Adela speaks to him about marriage before they enter the Marabar caves) immediately emerges as a supremely vital, sympathetic character. The reader, having listened to talk about the insults the Indians have to suffer, next witnesses an actual example involving Aziz. Thus before the crucial scene in the mosque with Mrs. Moore, which will be discussed in some detail in a later section, Aziz has been plunged into an atmosphere of jocular resentment, next subjected to the double indignity of receiving a peremptory summons from the Civil Surgeon who was out when he arrived, and of standing by while two English women commandeer his carriage. He is hardly well prepared to love the English and yet he gives his heart to Mrs. Moore on sight.

(iii) English in India: 'India does wonders for the judgment'

Although we hear something of the English officials through the dialogue between Aziz and his friends and meet Mrs. Callendar, Mrs. Lesley, and Mrs. Moore in the second chapter, our formal introduction to the life at the civil station does not occur until the third chapter. The cultural life, such as it is, is a trivial echo of the more superficial aspects of metropolitan culture; putting on 'Cousin Kate' is merely one example of the general attempt to reproduce English middle-class life in India. Daily activities have stultified into a dull routine, a meaningless, arid ritual, over which Mr. Turton, the Collector, benevolently presides. We are made acutely conscious of the deficiencies of the life at the civil station through the disappointment and boredom of the two newcomers, Mrs. Moore and Adela Quested.

In this club scene the main characters, without deteriorating into cardboard cut-outs or stereotypes, quickly identify themselves and announce their respective attitudes to life through particular phrases. Forster is always sensitive to 'voice'. Some key phrases are repeated as they are in a musical composition. The phrase 'I want to see the *real* India' partly explains Adela's presence in Chandrapore and exactly catches her rather humourless, earnest response to experience. The more down-to-earth, humorous attitude of Fielding, the Headmaster of the English college, is epitomised in 'Try seeing Indians'. The views of the English wives range from thoughtless stupidity through well-intentioned but obtuse advice, to Mrs. Callendar's callous, 'Why, the kindest thing one can do to a native is to let him die'. Once again one of the views put forward in the dialogue between the three Indians in II (that the women are worse than the men) seems to be confirmed by our subsequent experience, but most readers will feel that the presentation of these women verges so closely on caricature that they seem far less real than Mrs. Moore or Adela, or even Turton. It is a weakness that while he shows the stultifying limitations of English life in India sympathetically through Adela, Forster's attitude to the English officials' wives is one of uncompassionate contempt. At a first reading we may easily miss the subtle ironies that play about the Turtons' opinions of Adela. Mrs. Turton 'trusted that she hadn't been brought out to marry nice little Heaslop, though it looked like it'.

> Her husband agreed with her in his heart, but he never spoke against an Englishwoman if he could avoid doing so, and he only said that Miss Quested naturally made mistakes. He added: 'India does wonders for the judgment, especially during the hot weather. . . .'

There is a wealth of thematic irony condensed in these lines. Later Turton is appalled at Fielding's suggestion that Miss Quested could have made a mistake in accusing Aziz, and his bland faith in the hot weather is proved to have remarkably little substance.

We may wonder why Ronny's entrance is so long delayed in the novel. By the time he appears in the Club we have heard a good deal about him from various people; from the lawyers who plead in his court, from Mrs. Moore, from Turton, who notes with approval that he is 'a sahib; he's one of us', thus unconsciously exposing the shallow standards by which British officials judge people. This technique of building up Ronny's character through the comments of other people allows Forster to indicate his deficiencies while at the same time retaining sufficient sympathetic interest in him as Adela's suitor. Both she and Mrs. Moore become rapidly aware of the deterioration of character that has taken place since Ronny came to Chandrapore but to retain sufficient sympathy for Ronny as Adela's prospective husband, it is essential that his imperfections shou' emerge most clearly through the accounts of his enemies an not through Mrs. Moore's and Adela's comments, frank as thes often are.

The claustrophobic limitations of the English Club become immedi ately apparent; they are the limitations of the English community as whole. But there are indications that the society is not so irredeemabl bad as it at first seems. Not everyone subscribes to the narrow unthinkin standards conveniently epitomised in the single word 'pukka'. For example, when Mrs. Moore reflects, 'Let me think—we don't see the other side of the moon out here, no', a pleasant voice says:

> 'Come, India's not as bad as all that.' . . . 'Other side of the earth, if you like, but we stick to the same old moon.' Neither of them knew the speaker nor did they ever see him again. He passed with his friendly word through red-brick pillars into the darkness.

This incident parallels the appearance of Mrs. Moore beneath the pillars in the mosque (II) and suggests that intuitive kindness exists even within the English Club; it is an echo of Mrs. Moore's simple goodness, though at the much lower level of club bonhomie. Moreover Fielding, although as yet he hardly exists as a character, speaks with a highly individual voice. His remark about the necessity of seeing Indians if one is to see the real India introduces a breath of fresh air into the oppressive club atmosphere.

(b) INVITATIONS

(i) Personal. Aziz and Mrs. Moore, 'the secret understanding of the heart'

When Aziz and Mrs. Moore meet in the mosque both are seeking to escape from an alien environment. Aziz, who has been snubbed by Major Callendar and his wife, comforts himself with the thought of 'shaking the dust of Anglo-India off his feet'. Mrs. Moore wanders out into the moonlit night to seek relief from the heat and to avoid having to sit through a stage comedy she has already seen in London. For Aziz the beauty of the mosque, the complex duality of light and shade, and the building's power to bring to mind Islam (for him a complete and satisfactory way of life) releases his imaginative powers. Characteristically his moment of extreme happiness in finding someone else, an English-woman, who knows how he feels, arouses a protective possessiveness as well as a heartfelt desire to share his happiness with others. A similar possessiveness appears when he praises the native architecture of Fielding's house (VII) and when he presides over the picnic that he has arranged at the Marabar caves. When Forster describes Aziz's tearful repetition of the phrase 'the secret understanding of the heart', a phrase that Aziz hopes will form part of a Persian inscription on his own tomb, he is clearly suggesting that the Muslim doctor overvalues pathos, but it is this secret understanding that in fact brings the Indian and the old Englishwoman together.

It is appropriate that Mrs. Moore, who is to reveal an intuitive understanding of other people, 'ghosts', and spiritual realities, should be
introduced as a ghostly figure. She appears thus to Aziz's imagination,
which has been made acutely sensitive to any promise of beauty, love
and friendship by the associations of the mosque. Speaking first as a
disembodied voice (again one sees how important 'voice' is in Forster's
novels), she answers Aziz's angry strictures with simple explanations of
her conduct, after she has recovered from her initial shock at finding
someone in the mosque. Indeed her statement that she had removed her
shoes because 'God is here' is almost naïve in its simplicity. Once Aziz
discovers that the voice belongs to an old woman, 'a fabric bigger than
the mosque fell to pieces, and he did not know whether to be glad or
sorry'. If the sight of her dissolves a romantic dream, it also enables him
to speak to her as a person; as a result his subsequent behaviour is not
complicated by the sexual snobbery that so distresses Fielding, affects
his attitude towards women in general, and prevents him from being
magnanimous towards Adela over the question of compensation.

The focal centre of this chapter is the following passage:

> He was excited partly by his wrongs, but much more by the know-
> ledge that someone sympathized with them. It was this that led him
> to repeat, exaggerate, contradict. She had proved her sympathy by
> criticizing her fellow-countrywoman to him, but even earlier he had
> known. The flame that not even beauty can nourish was springing up,
> and though his words were querulous his heart began to glow secretly.
> Presently it burst into speech.
> 'You understand me, you know what others feel. Oh, if others
> resembled you!'
> Rather surprised, she replied: 'I don't think I understand people
> very well. I only know whether I like or dislike them.'
> 'Then you are an Oriental.' (II)

Nothing that happens later wholly invalidates the understanding
achieved by these two dissimilar people. This moment of revelation—a
muted epiphany—is the novel's positive affirmation. It is subject to
endless qualification and challenge, but as if to emphasise its potential
durability, Forster includes a similar moment of intuitive understanding
between Aziz and Ralph in Chapter XXXVI and the repeated motif
'Then you are an Oriental' recalls vividly for Aziz and, of course, for
the reader the memory of this exquisite moment in the mosque.

The achievement of this bond of understanding between the aggrieved

Aziz and the warm-hearted, sympathetic Mrs. Moore, with her wonderful openness to life and capacity to accept people and events without prior rationalisation, is not presented at the expense of excluding all those elements that threaten personal relations later in the novel. They are all there: the conflicting and discordant sounds of English and Hindu life heard from within the mosque, the hostility of nature suggested by the talk of dangerous snakes, the difficulty of communication hinted at in Aziz's mistaken idiom—'in the same box' for 'in the same boat'. Most striking of all is the confusion of names and identities that arises from Mrs. Moore's second marriage. This prefigures Aziz's tragic blunder about the identity of Fielding's wife in the last section of the book. By that time suspicion has triumphed over generous impulse. In the mosque, however, overflowing kindness creates new understanding from confusion. The fact that so much of the novel's complex thematic structure should be reflected in a single chapter points to the intense imaginative process that is at work.

(ii) Social. 'Bridge party' and Fielding's tea-party

The conversation between Aziz and his friends in the second chapter and the introduction to the Club develop a strong contrast between the casualness of Indian social intercourse and the rigid formality of English institutional life. The scene in the mosque marks the success of informal personal relations while the 'bridge party' arranged by Turton signalises the inevitable failure of all formal attempts to organise better understanding between different people. Communication is difficult. Mrs. Turton, who can only speak a few phrases of Urdu suitable for addressing servants, is surprised that some Indian women can speak English and have travelled in Europe—' "They pass Paris on the way no doubt," said Mrs. Turton, as if she was describing the movements of migratory birds.' And she fears that they may apply Western standards to her own conduct. Nevertheless even where officialdom, suspicion, shyness and the barrier of language keep the rulers and the ruled rigidly apart, spontaneous kindness throws a bridge across the gulf. Difference of language does not seriously handicap those who are unaffected by class and race arrogance, however. Mrs. Moore's proposal to visit Mrs. Bhattacharya gives genuine pleasure as do Fielding's gestures of friendship, but an emotional or aesthetic idea of truth similar to Aziz's prevents Mr. Bhattacharya from ruining a moment of happiness by admitting that he and his wife would be on their way to Calcutta. There is a strong contrast between the extreme delicacy and indirectness of the Indians and the brusque perfunctory gestures of the English officials. It is the attitude of the latter that destroys the possibility of the bridge party's success. Once again, as in Mahmoud Ali's comments on Mrs. Turton in II, one feels that Forster holds the women chiefly to blame.

Forster's language ironically mocks the godlike pretensions of the leaders of both people. The presiding deities on each side are Mr. Turton, the Collector, and the Nawab Bahadur. Forster suggests an ironic connection between the meeting at the tea-party and the meeting in the mosque by referring to the English Club as a 'shrine'. This implied criticism of the English officials is further developed when Adela quietly rebukes Ronny for his complacent arrogance, saying 'Your sentiments are those of a god', and again much later when, after the arrest of Aziz, the watching Turton is 'revealed like a god in a shrine'.

If there is a slight tendency for the social comedy in the bridge party to deteriorate into satiric caricature, this is partly offset by the complexity of the motives attributed to Turton in arranging the event and to the visitors in accepting. The less praiseworthy thoughts and motives of the Indians are more sympathetically presented than those of the English. Their inferior social status seems to justify a certain degree of pettiness and suspicion. The following passage reveals how carefully Forster distinguishes between the different reactions to Turton's invitation.

> Many of the guests, especially the humbler and less anglicized, were genuinely grateful. To be addressed by so high an official was a permanent asset. They did not mind how long they stood, or how little happened, and when seven o'clock struck, they had to be turned out. Others were grateful with more intelligence. The Nawab Bahadur, indifferent for himself and for the distinction with which he was greeted, was moved by the mere kindness that must have prompted the invitation. He knew the difficulties. Hamidullah also thought that the Collector had played up well. But others, such as Mahmoud Ali, were cynical; they were firmly convinced that Turton had been made to give the party by his official superiors and was all the time consumed with impotent rage, and they infected some who were inclined to a healthier view. Yet even Mahmoud Ali was glad he had come. Shrines are fascinating, especially when rarely opened, and it amused him to note the ritual of the English club, and to caricature it afterwards to his friends.

Where motives are so complex it is not surprising that muddle and misunderstanding ensue.

In strong contrast to this failure of officialdom to bridge the gulf between East and West is the success of the tea-party at the Government College. It is presided over by Fielding, a benevolent educator, a liberal humanist, a Ulysses who 'had seen too many cities and men' to be corrupted by the shallow wisdom of British officialdom in India. The party is preceded by an amusing and strangely moving scene in which kindness and good nature prevail in spite of misunderstanding, just as they had prevailed when Mrs. Moore and Aziz met in the mosque. Aziz's impulsiveness breaks down Fielding's English reserve and a bond of friendship is swiftly established. But the gift of the collar stud is presented on the level of social comedy; there is none of that deliberate heightening and intensifying of the imaginative atmosphere that makes the scene in the mosque a kind of epiphany. The bond between the Indian and the Englishman is continuously threatened as a result of failures in understanding. Here, as an ironic prelude to a successful experiment in personal relations, the reader is reminded of the unforeseen difficulties that beset all human communications. In a variety of ways we are made to see how easy it is for one person to misjudge another. For example, Ronny's later comment on Aziz's lack of a collar stud—'there you have the Indian all over: inattention to detail; the fundamental slackness that reveals the race', shows that preconceived notions determine judgements (VIII). But it is not only the British officials that make such snap judgements. We reduce the whole complexity of this scene if we fail to notice that Aziz judges the Bhattacharyas just as harshly and with just as little justice—'Slack Hindus—they have no idea of society.' It is a judgement that might more appropriately be applied to himself; ironically Aziz repeats the Battacharyas's mistake and is horrified to find that Adela has taken his invitation to his house seriously.

Amid the multiple misunderstandings, generosity and spontaneous affection prevail at the private tea-party. As if Aziz's volatile loquacity were infectious, Adela inadvertently lets slip a revealing remark. In answer to the Indian's question 'Why not settle altogether in India?' she says simply 'I'm afraid I can't do that'. Subsequently she realises that the remark implied a rejection of Ronny as a husband and should therefore have been made to him in the first place. The Indian's simple directness penetrates social reserve and personal reticence and evokes a truth of which Adela had not previously been conscious. Disguise and self-deception become more difficult to sustain in Aziz's company. In a similar fashion at the mouth of the caves, conversation about marriage with Aziz brings about the sudden realisation that, although she has agreed to marry Ronny, she does not love him.

One further way in which the conversation at the tea-party foreshadows the fuller working out of major themes is the introduction of the question whether India is a mystery or a muddle. Minor qualifications are made by some speakers, but on the whole it is true to say that the topic neatly divides the rationalists (Adela and Fielding) from the others. Mrs. Moore says, 'I like mysteries but I rather dislike muddles.' It is a very simple natural comment in its context, but it gathers round it complex associations. In different ways, Mrs. Moore and Godbole possess the necessary spiritual and imaginative powers to admit that there are mysteries that lie outside the comprehension of their finite minds.

(iii) Divine. Professor Godbole, 'Come, come, come'

The theme of man's relationship with his fellow man is linked to the theme of his relationship with the divine through the recurrent idea of 'invitation'. In neither sphere can perfect harmony be reached without some form of invitation and the two spheres are shown to be inter-related. Although the author scrupulously refrains from affirming the actual existence of a divine principle, he creates a wide variety of scenes to reveal that all human attempts to initiate unity, whether it be through intimate conversation or public meeting or private tea-party, fail because such attempts ignore the existence of forces outside man himself. The finite must come to terms with the infinite, Forster seems to suggest; hence the importance of imagination. His ironic descriptions of human behaviour reduce the stature of the characters; on many occasions direct commentary specifically relates their noble but pathetic attempts to the challenge of the infinite. The most striking occurs at the end of Chapter IV where Forster speaks of 'humanity grading and drifting beyond the educated vision, until no earthly invitation can embrace it'. He adds tentatively 'All invitations must proceed from heaven perhaps; perhaps it is futile for men to initiate their own unity, they do but widen the gulfs between them by the attempt.' Of course for Forster 'heaven' is simply a convenient label for whatever it is that his rational humanism cannot explain. The phrase 'little ineffectual unquenchable flames!' that describes the gestures of goodwill made by Aziz's friends around his sick-bed epitomises the tensions that are reconciled in Forster's complex vision. He is simultaneously aware of the finite and infinite in man's nature.

In various ways most of the major characters are seeking to escape
from the sense of being alone in an alien universe. They feel the human
need to escape from their separateness through love and friendship and
they yearn for some relationship with the divine. But their desires are
largely frustrated, and it is this which gives the novel a deep underlying
sadness beneath the brilliant social comedy, a sadness that is only
occasionally dispelled by the visionary glimpses of perfect unions,
human and divine.

Forster maintains a delicate balance between the romantic idea of the
imagination's power to penetrate ultimate reality and the sceptical
humanistic view that recognises the essential alienness of the natural
world. Thus when Aziz delights his companions with a vision of the
unity of Islam, the commentary reminds the reader of the existence of
'a hundred Indias' and of 'the indifferent moon'. In a series of imaginative
transfigurations, Aziz and Mrs. Moore separately and together sense the
unity of all creation. These visions are so bound up with their meeting
in the mosque that the ideas of human understanding and of discovering
beauty in the universe become inextricably related. Only through
imaginative perception of beauty and through love can we understand
other people and the universe in which we live. The capacity to respond
to beauty and to other people is shown to have a common source. The
connection, ideas of which may be traced to the Cambridge philosopher
G. E. Moore and to Goldsworthy Lowes Dickinson, is made most
explicitly in the haunting passage that describes Mrs. Moore's vision of
the beauty of the Indian night as she leaves the club with Adela and
Ronny (III).

> Mrs. Moore, whom the club had stupefied, woke up outside. She
> watched the moon, whose radiance stained with primrose the purple
> of the surrounding sky. In England the moon had seemed dead and
> alien; here she was caught in the shawl of night together with earth
> and all the other stars. A sudden sense of unity, of kinship with
> the heavenly bodies, passed into the old woman and out, like water
> through a tank, leaving a strange freshness behind. She did not dis-
> like 'Cousin Kate' or the National Anthem, but their note had died
> into a new one. . . . When the mosque, long and domeless, gleamed at
> the turn of the road, she exclaimed, 'Oh, yes—that's where I got
> to—that's where I've been.'

Here, as a natural part of Mrs. Moore's vision, images of moon, flowing
water, the tank, and mosque become associated with the promise of

harmony. A little later, in the same chapter, the radiant promise is described: it belonged 'neither to water nor to moonlight, but stood like a luminous sheaf upon the fields of darkness'. Reminiscent of the allusion in Chapter I to the 'branches and beckoning leaves' that make a 'city for the birds', these passages offer brief glimpses of a harmony that transcends the distinction between the finite earth and infinity.

The radical difference between Ronny's and Mrs. Moore's response to the beauty of the night is neatly underlined in his insensitive common-sense peremptory attitude when he calls his servant—'Going to the verandah, he called firmly to the moon. His sais answered, and without lowering his head, he ordered his trap to be brought round.' Through this subtle parallel and that with Professor Godbole (literally meaning 'sweet talker') invoking the god Krishna to 'Come, come, come', Forster establishes the connection between the capacity to love and the imaginative power to apprehend beauty and infinity.

The idea that all invitations must proceed from heaven, or must at least be prompted by a recognition of man's dependence on powers greater than himself, is first introduced in an ironic context. At the end of Chapter IV, Forster ridicules the limitations of the Christian missionaries, Mr. Graysford and Mr. Sorley. The irony is rather heavy-handed, but it serves the serious purpose of measuring the exclusiveness of Christianity by the inclusiveness of Hinduism. 'And the wasps? He [Mr. Sorley] became uneasy during the descent to wasps, and was apt to change the conversation.' Our appreciation of the novel's complex structure is enhanced if we remember this detail, since it picks up Mrs. Moore's simple loving acceptance of the wasp seen on the peg when she went to hang up her cloak, and foreshadows Professor Godbole's almost divine intuition when he impels the separate images of a wasp and of Mrs. Moore into a single act of consciousness (XXXIII). This climactic moment in 'Temple' has been well prepared for earlier in the novel. At the tea-party at the Government College, Godbole in spite of Ronny's brash, insensitive interruption sings a religious song, which is an 'invitation' to the divine, the lord of the universe, to come not simply to him but to the whole world. The description of the song as 'the song of an unknown bird' and of its effect on the man who 'came naked out of the tank, his lips parted with delight, disclosing a scarlet tongue' suggests Godbole's attunement to the mystery of the universe and that his experience may be shared even by the unlearned. A similar elevation of the 'primitive' appears in the description of the punkah wallah in the trial scene. Naturally enough Godbole's song to Krishna is not fully intelligible to people who cannot understand anything until they have classified and 'labelled' it. Through the image of the 'unknown bird', this passage is later linked in the reader's mind with the account of Adela's and Ronny's earnest but futile attempts to identify an Indian bird as they struggle to rationalise their relationship, to argue whether they should get married or not. It is also linked with Adela's fear of being 'labelled' should she become Ronny's wife, with the unknown animal that bumped into the Nawab Bahadur's car, and with the central mystery of what happened in the cave. By implication Godbole's imaginative apprehension of the infinite, his acquiescence in negation, is contrasted with the limitations of Western rationalism. Through these repeated motifs and interrelated scenes, Forster places the themes of personal and social invitation within a cosmic perspective.

(c) PERSONAL RELATIONS

(i) Adela and Ronny

Although in thematic structure and narrative technique A Passage to India is strikingly original, it retains many of the conventions of the traditional novel, the most obvious being the retention of a romantic plot in a vestigial form. Ronny Heaslop has commissioned (the word signifies his public attitude to private affairs) his mother to bring Adela to India. Much of the action before the disastrous picnic at the Marabar caves is concerned with Ronny and Adela. These episodes are integral to the larger themes of the book, since Adela's doubts about marrying Ronny spring from the recognition of the changes India has wrought in him and from her own failure to come to terms with what she calls 'the real India', or what we might call the real complexity of life.

Lacking any of the attributes of the conventional heroine, Adela possesses sufficient intellectual honesty and sincerity to make her an interesting and fairly sympathetic character. The typical bloodlessness of the Forsterian woman is not here a weakness. From the start, it appears unlikely that she will in fact marry Ronny. She herself is disturbed by the changes that India has brought about in his character: Mrs. Turton, who here represents the judgement of the British wives, thinks Adela is not 'pukka' and that she should marry Fielding, who is also not 'pukka'. Ronny is anxious that his future wife should start straight on the Indian question. Having abandoned the inquiry himself, he expects Adela to accept his ready-made, second-hand views on India, just as he had accepted them from his superior Turton (again and again his phrases echo Turton's). It is useless for Mrs. Moore to remind him that Adela's main purpose in coming out to India was to make up her own mind. 'She knows you in play, as she put it, but not in work, and she felt she must come and look round, before she decided—and before you decided. She is very fair-minded.' After the inevitable failure of the bridge party, Adela's fear that she would always 'see India as a frieze, never as a spirit' is confirmed, while her kindness to the Bhattacharyas and to Aziz convinces Ronny that she does not yet know how to behave in India.

The relations between Adela and Ronny reach a crisis after Fielding's tea-party. Adela, angry at Ronny's rudeness and her own inadequacy, deliberately provokes him in an angry scene when the subject of the visit to the caves is raised. She knows, as she casually announces the details, that Ronny will disapprove, but the intensity of his disapproval can hardly be explained simply in terms of race prejudice and social etiquette. Although neither Adela nor Ronny would be able to admit into their conscious minds that Aziz could be sexually attractive to an Englishwoman, the reader is already aware that the young Indian possesses just that vitality and human warmth which Ronny lacks. Forster makes no direct reference to sexual jealousy, except in early manuscript notes, in which the physical attraction between Adela (called Janet at this stage of the book's genesis) and Aziz is explicitly stated. Even though such details are not included in the final text, most readers will feel that unconscious sexual jealousy is one of the many sources of misunderstanding between these two very English lovers. Adela is shocked that 'Instead of weighing Ronny and herself, and coming to a reasoned conclusion about marriage, she had incidentally, in the course of a talk about mangoes, remarked to mixed company that she didn't mean to stop in India.' In other words, she has been temporarily influenced by Aziz's impulsive temperament—Aziz, who later protests against the English habit of thinking of emotions as something like potatoes to be 'weighed'. At Fielding's tea-party Adela has acted uncharacteristically in response to the stimulus of Aziz and to a new environment. In the scene on the Maidan, Ronny and Adela revert to their normal modes of behaviour, acting rationally, politely and with consideration for each other's feelings. But much has been going on in Adela's conscious and subconscious mind, and she announces her decision not to become engaged simply and with almost maternal tenderness:

> 'It's something very different, nothing to do with caves, that I wanted to talk over with you.' She gazed at the colourless grass. 'I've finally decided we are not going to be married, my dear boy.'

These words reveal her limited self-knowledge, since her thoughts about Aziz's invitation and the forthcoming visit to the caves are in fact both related to her recognition that she cannot marry Ronny. It is, I think, the sudden release of this suppressed awareness as she enters a Marabar cave that partly accounts for her belief that she had been attacked by Aziz and for her hysterical breakdown in the second main section of the novel.

The civilised reasonableness with which this English couple settles differences is immediately challenged and reduced in importance by being set against the background of the irrational and mysterious Indian world where the little green bird cannot be labelled and 'the mere asking of a question causes it to disappear or to merge into something else'. As in the later interview between Adela and Fielding after the trial, here also Ronny and Adela are reduced to dwarf-like stature. Thus even after the 'animal thrill' in the Nawab Bahadur's car has brought them closer together and the shared excitement of their Boy Scout-like tracking expedition has restored their good spirits, preparing the way for their decision to become engaged after all, the reader is very conscious of the 'spuriousness' of their unity, that it is an escape from an alien world and that it is too precarious to survive the mysterious threats of the dark, ominous, ghostly Indian scene. The central irony of Chapter VIII is that for all the lovers' common-sense rationalism, it is the forces of unreason that bring them together. Because neither has learnt to 'connect', to unite head and heart, reason and emotion, each is surprised when Adela asks to withdraw what she had said and they decide to become engaged.

> Neither had forseen such a consequence. She had meant to revert to her former condition of important and cultivated uncertainty, but it had passed out of her reach at its appropriate hour. Unlike the green bird or the hairy animal, she was labelled now. She felt humiliated again, for she deprecated labels, and she felt too that there should have been another scene between her lover and herself at this point, something dramatic and lengthy. He was pleased instead of distressed, he was surprised, but he had really nothing to say. What indeed is there

to say? To be or not to be married, that was the question, and they had decided it in the affirmative.

Both have what Forster calls in some 'Notes on the English Character' in *Abinger Harvest* 'an undeveloped heart—not a cold one. The difference is important.' Their idea of personal relations, though it is based on mutual respect, is too limited. Nothing warm and durable can be created from Adela's pathetic belief in worrying her way through to the truth nor from Ronny's conventional acceptance of marriage as social institution. Adela's feeling of humiliation arises from her fear that she has compromised her integrity in consenting to become labelled, her disappointment from her unsatisfied desire for emotional intensity and excitement. What should have been a moment of great happiness is clouded by guilt and self-reproach, feelings that break out again as she enters the Marabar cave.

The two lovers are too unimaginative to sense the strength of the forces that threaten their relationship from within and without. The prosaic dialogue underlines how very 'British' they are, an aspect of their behaviour that causes Adela some momentary doubt—' "We've been awfully British over it, but I suppose that's all right" ', but which causes Ronny none. But it is the author's voice, sometimes compassionate, sometimes ironic, that indicates the frailty of the human bond that links the lovers; Forster's evocation of the atmosphere of the Indian night powerfully suggests the areas of human experience that lie outside the lovers' consciousnesses. In one passage he questions the durability not only of this but of all human relationships.

> Her hand touched his, owing to a jolt, and one of the thrills so frequent in the animal kingdom passed between them, and announced that all their difficulties were only a lovers' quarrel. Each was too proud to increase the pressure, but neither withdrew it, and a spurious unity descended on them, as local and temporary as the gleam that inhabits a firefly. It would vanish in a moment, perhaps to reappear, but the darkness is alone durable. And the night that encircled them, absolute as it seemed, was itself only a spurious unity, being modified by the gleams of day that leaked up round the edges of the earth, and by the stars.

Such passages as these reduce human pretensions to insignificance. Human passion is shared with the animal kingdom and is ephemeral. Death alone is durable. Yet it is characteristic of Forster's commentary that its poetic quality should qualify the force of the negative vision.

(ii) *Aziz and Fielding*

The relationship between Aziz and Fielding, not that between Adela and Ronny, is the main focus of interest in the novel. Both of course illustrate the difficulties that beset personal relations, but the friendship between the two men more adequately shows the complex tensions between East and West and the limits of human communication.

When Fielding and Aziz are first brought together in the novel (VII), the character of the English schoolmaster has not yet been established. His earlier career is rather awkwardly outlined. Aziz and his friends have instantly sprung to life because they have been introduced more informally and dramatically. In contrast, the brief sketch seems lifeless and intrusive, as do similar sketches in Hardy. To some readers the sentence 'His career, though scholastic, was varied, and had included going to the bad and repenting thereafter' may appear an ironic echoing of conventional phrasing; to others it may suggest that Forster has not imagined very deeply this aspect of Fielding's life. Later perfunctory references to this episode add nothing to its reality. Prim, ironic, Meredithian overtones sound an unreal note: 'There needs must be this evil of brains in India, but woe to him through whom they are increased.' However these minor infelicities should not prevent readers from recognising the crucial importance of the introductory account of Fielding. A mature, middle-aged man, he has the breadth of experience that the English officials lack. Like his creator, he has come to India after living in Italy. He 'often attempted analogies between this peninsula and that other, smaller and more exquisitely shaped that stretches into the classic waters of the Mediterranean'. Like his creator's, his attitude towards Englishwomen in India is antipathetic. Fielding has all the virtues of the liberal humanist: he believes in the supreme value of ideas, is free from race feeling, remains detached, observant, sceptical, tolerant amid an intolerant passionate environment. Here, then, is a man apparently ideally suited to prove that the world 'is a globe of men who are trying to reach one another and can best do so by the help of good will plus culture and intelligence' (VII). Little irony qualifies Forster's expression of this faith. It is only later that we are made to realise the limitations of such a creed and of the man who professes it—that he is unable to give himself wholly to anyone, that his imagination is too undeveloped to understand experiences that are not susceptible of purely rational explanation. For him mystery is synonymous with muddle. He 'travels light' at the expense of forming deeper, more permanent relations.

Commendably, like Adela, he does not wish to be 'labelled'. Unlike both Adela and Mrs. Moore, he is unable to develop the 'echo' at all. 'It belonged to the universe that he had missed or rejected.' A rationalist, he cannot admit the irrational, a positive man, he cannot accept the negative message of the caves. Fielding's outlook and experience parallel Forster's in a number of important respects. In an early manuscript version of the cave episode, he appears more responsive to poetry and more closely reflects the author's sensibility. In this version, Fielding, not Aziz, finds Ronny's field-glasses at the mouth of the cave; he falls into a dialogue with the echo, quotes Milton, Dante, and the Persian inscription Aziz has taught him. But in the printed text he ceases to be a projection of the author; Forster's knowledge of life has become more extensive, his imagination penetrates to levels inaccessible to Fielding's rational mind. In creating Fielding, Forster steps outside his own liberal humanistic creed, views it ironically, and recognises its limits.

The first meeting between Aziz and Fielding proves that good will, spontaneity, and generous impulses can temporarily bridge the great gulf—linguistic and cultural—that separates the two men. Nevertheless we are kept constantly aware of the imminent danger of a break-down in communication, which must produce misunderstanding, distrust and suspicion. Fielding's first remark, a completely formal greeting, 'Please make yourself at home', is mistaken for a sign of delightfully unconventional behaviour. A little later, Aziz interprets Fielding's jocular dismissal of Post-Impressionism as a personal snub, springing from the schoolmaster's race prejudice, a remark typical of English condescension. Fortunately Aziz's sense of Fielding's 'fundamental good will' is too strong to allow petty annoyance to spoil the moment. His own good will 'went out to it, and grappled beneath the shifting tides of emotion which alone bear the voyager to an anchorage but may carry him across it on to the rocks'. It is characteristic that the affirmation should immediately be qualified. Fielding's buoyant optimism, his relaxed manner help to avert a scene. The trouble with Aziz, as Forster remarks, is that he is 'sensitive rather than responsive. In every remark he found a meaning, but not always the true meaning, and his life though vivid was largely a dream.' Abundance of imagination rather than lack of it, as in Fielding's case, is Aziz's potential strength and besetting weakness; his 'dreams' easily become nightmares of ignoble suspicion. Obviously satisfactory relations between these two so dissimilar men would involve some Coleridgean balance and reconciliation of opposites.

The features of the Government College that specially charm Aziz are the beauty of the building and the gardens, the lack of formality (he does not find 'everything ranged coldly on shelves' as he expected), the kindness of Fielding and his guests, and the opportunity to lose himself in a dream of India's past glories. 'Wings bore him up, and flagging would deposit him.' The same image is used to suggest the oscillations of his volatile temperament at the Marabar caves. Excited, and on the spur of the moment, he invites Mrs. Moore and Adela to his house, only to regret it a minute later. He rhapsodises about justice and the beauty of Fielding's house; he points out, somewhat inarticulately and with a typical taint of possessiveness, the signs of loving craftsmanship in the college architecture. With scant respect for the laws of gravity, he connects the water in the garden with the water by 'our mosque' (the 'our' significantly includes Mrs. Moore in its joyous possessiveness). Water cannot flow up hill, but here truth of the heart, truth of the transfiguring imagination, is contrasted with mere verbal truth, a contrast that is developed in relation to Aziz throughout the novel.

The first meeting with the English schoolmaster leaves Aziz with the conviction that 'No Englishman understands us except Mr. Fielding'. Thus when Aziz, taken slightly ill with fever, is overwhelmed by self-pity and the need for love, his thoughts turn to Fielding. Wondering how he will manage to see his new friend, he imagines his shame if Fielding were to visit his squalid, fly-ridden house. Fielding does in fact come. He arrives in the middle of a conversation between Aziz and his Indian friends, a conversation that expresses a complex blend of genuine affection, mutual suspicion and pettiness. Dislike of the English creates a spurious unity. 'As long as someone abused the English all went well', but the attitude of the Hindu doctor Panna Lal indicates that the gulf between Muslim and Hindu is as deep as that between the Indians and the English. (Intelligent Hindus still find it difficult to forgive Forster for making his 'hero' a Muslim, but in earlier versions he was even more of an 'outsider', having been a medical student in Germany, with an interest in fencing, riding and physical culture.) Throughout the bedside scene, Forster maintains a delicate balance between comedy and compassion; the details of Godbole's illness are purely comic, but the treatment of the absurdities of Aziz's visitors is deeply tinged with compassion. When Hamidullah, his mind full of the contrast between the peace of Cambridge and the warring factions of Chandrapore, says goodbye, it becomes a strangely moving scene.

'I shall not forget those affectionate words,' replied Aziz.

'Add mine to them,' said the engineer.

'Thank you, Mr. Syed Mohammed, I will.'

'And mine,' 'And, sir, accept mine,' cried the others, stirred each according to his capacity towards good will. Little ineffectual unquenchable flames!

The last comment, apart from epitomising the essential tension between affirmation ('unquenchable') and retraction ('ineffectual') which is reconciled in Forster's vision, prevents the Indian characters from becoming merely ridiculous.

In Chapters IX, X and XI we observe Forster's great skill in ironic composition. Aziz shows Fielding his dead wife's photograph. This is one of the novel's most moving expressions of friendship, and it is set in a context that simultaneously dramatises its poignant nobility and its essentially fragile nature. When Fielding first arrives unobserved (IX) in the middle of the silly quarrel about Godbole's mysterious illness, there seems no possibility of any deep understanding between the Indian doctor and the English schoolmaster. Once he begins to speak, Fielding's frank, humorous excuse for being in India, like his remarks on the growing disbelief in God among educated thoughtful people, leaves the Indians bewildered.

> The line of thought was not alien to them, but the words were too definite and bleak. Unless a sentence paid a few compliments to Justice and Morality in passing, its grammar wounded their ears and paralysed their minds. What they said and what they felt were (except in the case of affection) seldom the same.

As polite farewells are exchanged, the collapse of communication seems complete.

As if to emphasise the futility and insignificance of all attempts to achieve human understanding, Forster interposes a brief atmospheric chapter (X) that powerfully suggests the dehumanising effect of the imminent hot weather. Consequently the understanding reached by Fielding and Aziz in the next chapter (XI) appears precarious and insubstantial, doubly so since the sun is shown as inimical to all human effort, not as the 'unattainable' nor the 'eternal promise' that haunts our consciousness, and because Aziz has come to substitute patronage for his original admiration for Fielding. He has found the Englishman imprudent in his too frank conversation. Nevertheless, Aziz showing his wife's photograph cements the bond of friendship. Because Muslims allow such privileges only to close relatives, the gesture assumes sacramental status, symbolising their 'brotherhood', and is in ironic contrast to Turton's act of showing an Indian lawyer his stamp album as a gesture of friendship (II).

The two men are strongly drawn to each other, but the reader is made continuously aware of differences in character and outlook. Fielding cannot be carried away on waves of emotion as Aziz can; consequently he cannot give himself whole-heartedly to this or to any relationship, nor can he believe that India's complex problems can be solved through 'Kindness, kindness, and more kindness.' The description of the photograph recalls realities Aziz chooses to ignore and connects the gesture of 'brotherhood' to the challenge offered by the enigmatic 'echo' in the caves. 'The lady faced the world at her husband's wish and her own, but how bewildering she found it, the echoing contradictory world.' Economically the device not only links 'brotherhood' and 'echo' but suggests the difference in sexual and family *mores*. This is more fully developed in the dialogue when discussions of marriage and pride in parenthood produce misunderstanding between the two. It is often by such apparently trivial details in the dialogue as Aziz's 'She has practically no breasts' and the comment on Fielding's response, 'He smiled too, but found a touch of bad taste in the reference to a lady's breasts', that Forster most successfully conveys the difficulties of communication between people of different cultures. In an earlier version of this conversation, the remark produced violent race revulsion in Fielding; in the printed text it is more appropriately made a question of taste.

In spite of all difficulties and misunderstandings, the first section 'Mosque' ends with the triumph of affection. Aziz drops asleep

amid the happier memories of the last two hours—poetry of Ghalib, female grace, good old Hamidullah, good Fielding, his honoured wife and dear boys. He passed into a region where these joys had no enemies but bloomed harmoniously in an eternal garden, or ran down watershoots of ribbed marble, or rose into domes whereunder were inscribed, black against white, the ninety-nine attributes of God. (XI)

This last vision of untroubled harmony before the release of herd instincts and mass hysteria unobtrusively draws together the major images and themes of the first section of the novel. By this stage they have accumulated complex associations, but the first time they have all been brought together is as they form a pattern in Aziz's dissolving consciousness. By this means psychological realism and symbolic resonance are deftly fused. The quiet end is an ironic prelude to the tragedy to be enacted in the next main section 'Caves'.

3. Caves

(a) THE VISIT

(i) *The message of the caves, 'vision or nightmare?'*

The elaborately fanciful and slightly overwritten Chapter XII declares unmistakably that the story has entered a new phase. The visions of harmony with which 'Mosque' ended are dispelled by the poetic evocation of primeval India. Consequently the events that follow have already been placed within a vast geological perspective, a device that further diminishes man in the scale of being. The Marabar caves 'are older than all spirit'. In bringing his characters to the caves, Forster is confronting them at the symbolic level with a part of India—and indeed the universe —that is not allowed for in Western religions and philosophies of life. For the moment it may be said that the caves represent 'Negation' and that it assumes a different guise for each. Although it is the pre-human, alien, indefinable character of the caves that the writing stresses, the exquisite description of the flame and its reflection hints at a unity of spirit and flesh that everything associated with the caves seems to deny. By a subtle modulation from delight in sensuous beauty to regret at transience, the description assimilates the brief vision of beauty into the prevailing atmosphere of negation, darkness, and impending disaster, symbolised by the hollow rock, the Kawa Dol, swaying in the wind, about to fall at any minute. 'The radiance increases, the flames touch one another, kiss, expire. The cave is dark again, like all the caves.'

From now on chance plays an important part in the working out of events. The visit to the caves takes place by chance, Fielding misses the train because Godbole happens to misjudge the length of a prayer. This element, far from suggesting that men are victims of a malign fate as in Hardy, becomes part of the general muddle of India and is closely related to particular characters, to Aziz for example, who first finds it convenient to forget his invitation until he hears through servants' gossip that Adela and Mrs. Moore are disappointed and who then strives desperately to overcome his customary casualness in order to prove that Indians can be as punctual and efficient as their English masters. There is something touchingly comic about his decision to sleep at the station so as not to be late. The difficulties he encounters in planning the visit emphasise the gulfs that divide people in India, but they arise from something more than questions of eating habits and etiquette. 'Trouble after trouble encountered him, because he had challenged the spirit of the Indian earth, which tries to keep men in compartments.' Throughout the novel the disharmonies have both a social and a cosmic dimension. And the two interpenetrate.

The texture of the writing in Chapters XIII and XIV prompts the reader to look out for 'clues'. These operate at two levels: the realistic and symbolic. Clearly something disastrous is going to happen during the picnic. As in a detective story we seize on suspicious events, so here we are expected to note the details relating to the bribing of Antony the servant, the arrival at the caves, the entry, and Adela's sudden departure; and we are intended to assume that they have special significance. But much is unexplained. Suspense is necessary to achieve the sudden surprise of Aziz's arrest. At the deeper symbolic level the description of the journey to the caves, the account of the caves themselves, and of Mrs. Moore's reflections on the significance of the echo, create a sense of mystery that by its very nature cannot be dispelled or explained by reference to 'what really happened' any more than Wordsworth's intuitions of 'unknown modes of being' can. Although some readers, for example Forster's friend G. L. Dickinson, have felt frustrated because the author never says explicitly what took place in the cave, the decision to create mystery of plot was surely sound. The characters themselves offer tentative answers: a 'ghost', 'hallucination', the 'guide', but the reader is not intended to accept any of them as very satisfactory. An earlier account, which Forster wisely rejected, made it clear that Adela had in fact been attacked by an unknown assailant; in this version realistic narrative and symbolic structure were in danger of working against each other. The symbolic structure required that Adela like Mrs. Moore should be confronted with the 'unknown'; in Adela's case the unknown in the universe and within her own nature. To leave the question 'What happened in the cave?' open but to enable the reader finally to work out a plausible psychological explanation for Adela's conduct ensures that the details of the plot serve the symbolic meaning and that the ordinary reader is not left unsatisfied and bewildered. It may be, however, that for some readers such details as the broken field-glasses, which belong more closely to the discarded version, appear to promise a simple solution that is of course never given.

During the railway journey to the Marabar Hills, a journey that begins in an atmosphere of comic confusion and minor disaster, Adela's mind races ahead, making elaborate plans for the future. She delights in ordering her life along sensible rational lines, but lacks the imagination to realise that she and Ronny have caused inconvenience and discomfort for Mrs. Moore, who will not now be able to escape before the hot weather comes. A similar confidence in her rationality, coupled with plain inexperience of life, prevents her from understanding that some English wives who leave their 'husbands grilling on the plain' do so for the sake of the children and not from selfish motives. There is a strong contrast between Adela's immaturity and Mrs. Moore's sympathetic understanding of family duties. We are therefore hardly prepared for Mrs. Moore's sudden loss of faith in the importance of personal relations.

> She felt increasingly (vision or nightmare?) that, though people are important the relations between them are not, and that in particular too much fuss has been made over marriage; centuries of carnal embracement, yet man is no nearer to understanding man. And to-day she felt this with such force that it seemed itself a relationship, itself a person who was trying to take hold of her hand. (XIV)

At this stage in the narrative when Mrs. Moore feels that her duty to Ronny has been done, the changed attitude may seem mainly due to temporary dejection or momentary apathy. But it is clearly placed where it is before the 'message of the train' and the 'message of the caves' to suggest that her overwhelming psychic experience at the Marabar Hills has physical and psychological origins and is not simply a case of a mind temporarily unbalanced by an almost supernatural experience. Most important of all, the idea that her negative vision took the form of a 'person who was trying to take hold of her hand' prepares us for Adela's belief that Aziz had assaulted her. For Adela too, a negative vision (marriage without love) assumes a physical form that reaches out to possess her.

Forster, by interweaving commentary, description, and inner dialogue, makes us aware that Adela's too earnest pursuit of the exciting and the significant prevents her from understanding the 'message of the train'. She tries to connect the details of the landscape, the place where the hyena struck the Nawab Bahadur's car for example, with her own personal life, but she cannot admit into her consciousness a sense of the featureless monotony of the Indian scene, the absence of any direction or purpose. The commentary, too, stresses its elusive quality ('How can the mind take hold of such a country?'). It connects the Indian landscape with the theme of divine promise and with Professor Godbole's song at Fielding's tea-party, a song that expressed humble acquiescence in negation, an acceptance that lies quite outside Adela's rational approach to life—and, as we see later, somewhat outside Mrs. Moore's as well. India 'calls "Come" through her hundred mouths, through objects ridiculous and august. But come to what? She has never defined. She is not a promise, only an appeal.' When in fact the promise comes with the dawning day, it is a false promise:

> But at the supreme moment, when night should have died and day lived, nothing occurred. It was as if virtue had failed in the celestial fount.

Here, as elsewhere in the novel, the visionary moment is succeeded by disappointment, emptiness, negation, a kind of cosmic backwash that haunts the mind long after the novel has been finished.

In his delight at the success of his arrangements for the picnic, Aziz attains an almost regal stature, but as the guests first approach the hills on the elephant provided through his strenuous and devious efforts, a new quality in the landscape

> occurred, a spiritual silence which invaded more senses than the ear. Life went on as usual, but had no consequences, that is to say, sounds did not echo or thoughts develop. Everything seemed cut off at its root, and therefore infected with illusion.

This linking of the landscape with inner emptiness foreshadows Mrs. Moore's experience in the caves. None of its details can be labelled, there is uncertainty whether an object is a snake or a stick. The extreme subjectivity of truth is stressed; this anticipates the impossibility of saying what happened to Adela in the caves. 'Nothing was explained and yet there was no romance.' Not surprisingly everything connected with the picnic acquires an illusory quality: Aziz's possessive joy in his lavish hospitality, the memory of his shared happiness in the mosque, his identification of himself with the Emperor Babur, his visions of his heroic ancestors, talk of united India, universal brotherhood, marriage. By this creation of an atmosphere of illusion through landscape and by means of the circumstantial details of Mrs. Moore's unpleasant claustrophobic experience in one of the caves, the reader is carefully prepared for the old lady's nihilistic vision.

> The crush and the smells she could forget, but the echo began in some indescribable way to undermine her hold on life. Coming at a moment when she chanced to be fatigued, it had managed to murmur, 'Pathos, piety, courage—they exist, but are identical, and so is filth. Everything exists, nothing has value.'

In the long passage of which this is only a part, Forster symbolises the ineradicable evil, the negation that may lie at the heart of the universe. Through the consciousness of a kindly, sympathetic, old woman whose simple intuition of goodness and truth and whose capacity for 'wise passiveness' has been evident so far, we are presented with a nightmare vision that amounts to a challenge to Christianity and to the pretensions of the Western liberal mind.

(ii) *What happened at the caves*

A moment before Mrs. Moore experiences this terrifying sense of emptiness, she suggests that Aziz should continue the exploration of the caves without her; she thinks 'how good he was, and how deeply she desired his happiness'. It is ironical that this human reflection of divine love—desire for the happiness of another is presented most clearly as an aspect of the divine in Professor Godbole's religious exaltation at Mau—should precede religious disillusionment for Mrs. Moore and unhappiness for Aziz.

Aziz and Adela enter a cave, light a match, and admire the reflection, but there is no sense of rapport as there has been between Aziz and Mrs. Moore; and, in any case, both are preoccupied with their own thoughts, Aziz with thoughts about the breakfast arrangements, Adela with thoughts about Ronny. The sight of 'a double row of footholds' in a rock, by reminding Adela of the wheel tracks left by the Nawab Bahadur's car and therefore of the chance ride that brought the lovers finally together, brings a sudden recognition that she does not love her fiancé. Characteristically she experiences vexation rather than anything deeper at the idea that they have allowed 'esteem and animal contact at dusk' to be a substitute for love, love which alone connects the physical and the spiritual. Her habitual common sense represses further conscious thought about her discovery, but her first words to Aziz are about marriage. With her customary cool objectivity that only deserts her before the trial, she notes how handsome Aziz is, regrets that neither she nor Ronny has physical charm, then asks Aziz how many wives he has—an unintentionally insulting question to put to an emancipated Muslim. Since F. C. Crews has recently claimed that Adela is physically attracted to Aziz and subconsciously desires to be raped by him, it is worth pointing out that Forster specifically says that she 'did not admire him with any personal warmth', had 'nothing of the vagrant in her blood', and thought of his attraction only in terms of women of his own race. Her attitude is impersonal, patronising: 'handsome little Oriental', she thinks. At the moment Adela enters the cave, she has still failed to 'connect'—'thinking with half her mind "sight-seeing bores me", and wondering with the other half about marriage'. The simplest interpretation of Adela's belief that she has been attacked by Aziz is to say that it is an objectification of the intense emotional assault on her reason that she has tried vainly to suppress. She has tried to live by the mind and is ashamed that animal desires have brought her and Ronny together. The imagined assault is a reflection of her deeply divided being, of the unresolved battle of forces within her, and also of her lack of self-knowledge. We may think of the entry into the cave as perhaps representing a descent into the subconscious. Only after Adela has come to realise the limits of her rationality and has come to terms with her echo, is she certain that Aziz is innocent. What actually happened at the physical level, whether she suffered a moment of panic or whether a guide followed her, is of little importance. What is important is that we should feel that everything Adela stands for, British common sense, repression of emotions, instinct for compromise, is brought up against an overwhelming force with which it cannot come to terms. By means of this incident, the action that is necessary to provoke the sharpest conflict between East and West—the accusation of Aziz—is made to comprehend all the major themes of the novel: the need to connect body and spirit, the contrast between Western rationalism and the mystery of India, the failure of individuals to communicate one with another.

(b) CONSEQUENCES

(i) *The Arrest*

The first obvious consequence of the visit to the caves is the unexpected arrest of Aziz. 'Dr. Aziz, it is my highly painful duty to arrest you.' Fielding, who had eventually joined the picnic, who had sensed something wrong and annoyed Miss Derek and Mrs. Moore with his curt questions, now tries to persuade Aziz to behave like a common-sense Englishman who has been unjustly charged. Childishly absurd as the emotional Aziz's attempt to jump out on the other side of the railway carriage may seem, Fielding's reaction to the situation is equally inappropriate. From this moment onwards reason has little chance to prevail.

Turton, the Collector, takes no part in the arrest, but watches from the station waiting room 'like a god in a shrine'. When he speaks to Fielding, we witness the conflict between the Collector's deeply ingrained racial prejudice based on stock responses and Fielding's dispassionate interest in the truth. This is the prelude to the outburst of herd instincts, mass hysteria and evil, an outburst that reaches its climax at the trial. Although Fielding is confident that he will be able to establish Aziz's innocence as soon as he is able to talk to the more reasonable McBryde, the District Superintendent of Police, he fares no better in this second interview. Not much can be expected from a man who has a theory that 'all unfortunate natives are criminals at heart for the simple reason that they live south of latitude 30'. Moreover, McBryde has assembled an impressive collection of circumstantial evidence. But the discrepancy between the Police Superintendent's interpretation of the 'photographs of women' discovered in Aziz's house and Fielding's simple statement of the truth 'That's his wife', suggests forcefully how the most innocent aspects of Aziz's life are likely to be cynically misunderstood and misused in evidence from now on. Ironically, McBryde, this British moral bulldog, is later found to be unfaithful to his wife. Fielding is shocked that the Muslim doctor's private letters should be examined. Like Mrs. Moore earlier in the novel, he has the deepest respect for the privacy of the individual. Subsequently, however, when Aziz himself shows his willingness to read private letters from Ronny and Adela at Mau, Forster applies different standards and justifies his behaviour on two grounds: 'private correspondence has never been ratified in the east' and by excusing it on the grounds that McBryde had read Aziz's letters—a rare example of special pleading by the author.

The fight for Aziz's innocence is not as simple a matter as Fielding at first expected. Forster reveals great psychological insight and subtle narrative skill in exploring the complicated reactions to the arrest in the English and Indian communities. Fielding, having decided to throw in his lot with the Indians, expects to receive their full and unqualified support. But the cautious temporising lawyer Hamidullah on whom he calls does not respond as expected at all. When he does at last suggest a plan, it is designed to involve as many interests as possible and to exploit anti-British feelings. Events insidiously compel the free-minded Fielding to take sides, to consent to be 'labelled' anti-British. He regrets it, just as he regrets his involvement in the 'muddle' that must inevitably accompany his fight for justice in this environment.

Utterly distinct from Hamidullah's diplomatic caution and deviousness and Fielding's simple integrity is Professor Godbole's reaction to the news of the arrest. At first his conversation seems to represent only the maddening inconsequence of the Indian mind, as he asks Fielding to suggest a name for a new High School in his native province. As soon as Fielding, thoroughly exasperated, tries to pin him down with the straight question: 'Is Aziz innocent or guilty?' Godbole begins to speak of what has happened in terms of the Hindu philosophy of good and evil. For the Western reader his patient exposition supplies a necessary gloss on other important passages in the book, and the repetition of 'Come, come, come' links this passage with many others that offer 'invitations' to the divine. In answer to Fielding's complaint that he is saying that good and evil are the same, Godbole replies:

'Oh no, excuse me once again. Good and evil are different as their names imply. But, in my own humble opinion, they are both of them aspects of my Lord. He is present in the one, absent in the other, and the difference between presence and absence is great, as great as my feeble mind can grasp. Yet absence implies presence, absence is not non-existence, and we are therefore entitled to repeat, "Come, come, come, come." '

The passage helps to explain why Godbole can acquiesce in apparent negation while Mrs. Moore can not. The ironic handling of this whole interview underlines the contrast between Fielding's exasperation at his own impotence, his active engagement in Aziz's cause, and Godbole's serene detachment. As so often in this novel there is a very subtle blend of comedy and seriousness. The partly comic treatment of Godbole has the effect of dissociating what is most annoyingly human in him, his air of coy mysticism, from the serious doctrine he expounds. And yet the comedy also serves to qualify the truth of the doctrine itself. The author himself can clearly not subscribe whole-heartedly to it.

To complete the picture of the various reactions to the arrest, Chapter XIX ends with Fielding's visit to the prisoner. He finds him unapproachable through misery. ' "You deserted me," was his only coherent remark.' It is a pathetic cry that is to be re-echoed immediately after the trial. The consequences of the arrest, then, are complex and unpredictable. The rewards for Fielding's loyalty to Aziz are an accusation of desertion from the man he has sacrificed so much to save, and hatred and suspicion from the British, who regard his sense of evidence with respect to Aziz's case as perverse and disloyal.

(ii) The release of mass hysteria and evil

Chapter XX opens with a description of the effect of the arrest on the English women; it marks the beginning of the outbreak of mass hysteria. The sense of guilt at not having done more for the peculiar young Englishwoman Adela expresses itself in a gush of sentiment that is soon exhausted. Mrs. Turton visits her in the sick room, speaks of her sentimentally, but on recalling that she had formerly condemned Adela as not 'pukka', breaks down and cries. There is a brief outburst of spurious tenderness all round and a sense of guilt, but both soon vanish. There is no real fellowship in suffering; this would require imagination and love, both of which the women lack. A momentary reminder of the theme of 'invitation' indicates why they cannot share Adela's suffering.

> If she wasn't one of them, they ought to have made her one, and they could never do that now, she had passed beyond their invitation.

Purely formal social relations are here implicitly contrasted with Fielding's spontaneous kindness and selflessness based on a sense of brotherhood; they are also contrasted with the theme of divine 'invitation' adumbrated by Godbole.

Although parts of the club scene may seem unduly exaggerated and the characters in danger of becoming rather crude satiric caricatures, the total conception is made credible through the frequent references to herd instincts and mass hysteria. Moreover the attentive reader will pick up details that add ironic complexity to the general pattern. For example, he will note that the drunken subaltern praises the Indian with whom he played polo, unaware that it was in fact Aziz, the accused man, now the object of his wrath. Against the unreality of the emotions aroused by the arrest, Ronny's unaffected quietness of demeanour stands out and would give him a minor tragic stature, if he did not so obviously accept the role of social martyr. Once again Fielding finds himself in a compromising situation. He is a little ashamed of his own refusal to stand when Ronny enters. But he will not succumb to the herd instinct of the Club, he will not join in its formal gestures. His statement that Aziz is innocent is characteristically forthright and courageous, so too is his offer to resign. But this is neither the time nor the place for brave integrity. He is summarily dismissed by the Collector and propelled ignominiously from the room. Passion, prejudice, muddle, and herd instincts have prevailed. At the end of it all Fielding goes out on the verandah to regain his mental balance. He has seemed heroic, but he is immediately confronted by something that dwarfs him. The limitations of his liberal humanist mind emerge in his inability to respond to the sight of the Marabar Hills.

> It was the last moment of the light, and as he gazed at the Marabar Hills they seemed to move graciously towards him like a queen, and their charm became the sky's. At the moment they vanished they were everywhere, the cool benediction of the night descended, the stars sparkled, and the whole universe was a hill. Lovely, exquisite moment —but passing the Englishman with averted face and on swift wings. He experienced nothing himself; it was as if someone had told him there was such a moment, and he was obliged to believe.

Visions of beauty and romantic heroism, unknown spiritual forces, can find no permanent dwelling-place in his consciousness, since his mind is fixed on facts and he is confident that he will discover what really happened in the caves. Although incapable of experiencing anything significant as he looks at the hills, he is at least filled with a sense of disquiet and is dissatisfied with his life. As so often in this novel, personal inadequacy goes with insensitivity to beauty and to the infinite.

(iii) Mrs. Moore, 'Aziz is innocent'. Last vision of India

Between Fielding's resignation from the Club and the dramatic account of the trial, there are crucial chapters that evoke the changing atmosphere of the town (XXI), explore Adela's attitude to Aziz's guilt

(XXII), and describe India's final message to Mrs. Moore (XXIII). The brief Chapter XXI vividly suggests the effects on the Indian community of the increasing heat and the excited preparations for the festival of Mohurram. It is against this background of confusion that we are invited to see the campaign for the prisoner's defence in which Fielding is now deeply involved. Amid noise and distractions, he longs to tell Godbole of his 'tactical and moral error' in being rude to Ronny Heaslop at the Club. This is an indication that Godbole, fallible and slightly comic as he may be, appears to Fielding—and to some extent to the reader—as a standard of truth. His 'knack of slipping off' and his attitude of serene detachment make him unapproachable, however. He is as elusive and impenetrable as the visions of beauty and infinity that India offers. Yet he serves as a touchstone of reality.

When we are once more introduced to Adela, she is in a state of nervous collapse at the McBryde bungalow. Miss Derek and Mrs. McBryde, who attend her, only exacerbate her fear of physical touch by picking cactus spines from her flesh with the aid of magnifying glasses, a detail that neatly suggests a misplaced faith in scientific rationalism. Hitherto Adela has lived through her mind and neglected her body. For all her admirable qualities, she is not only unimaginative but deficient in emotion. Now her emotions have taken their revenge: everything is transferred to the surface of her body. But she retains enough of her former character to despise her own emotional outbursts. Her account of what happened at the caves is brief and unsatisfactory.

> 'I remember scratching the wall with my finger-nail, to start the usual echo, and then as I was saying there was this shadow, or sort of shadow, down the entrance tunnel, bottling me up. It seemed like an age, but I suppose the whole thing can't have lasted thirty seconds really. I hit at him with the glasses, he pulled me round the cave by the strap, it broke, I escaped, that's all. He never actually touched me once. It all seems such nonsense.'

One notices how the 'shadow' becomes personalised—'I hit at him'—without rational explanation. The one person Adela longs to see is Mrs. Moore (just as Fielding longs to see Godbole). A spiritual battle between the forces of good and evil rages within her; evil triumphs—'only Mrs. Moore could drive it back to its source and seal the broken reservoir'. The imagery of the sound that 'spouted after her . . . like a river that gradually floods the plain' and of 'reservoir' suggest the subsconscious.

Adela's breakdown is an effective method of dramatising her sudden confrontation by forces which she had not allowed for in her rational common-sense approach to life. Forster stresses that the echo, although it is unimportant intellectually, haunts her mind and permeates her whole being.

A letter to Adela from Fielding affirming Aziz's innocence produces a complex effect. At first it arouses indignation as she thinks of Fielding's rudeness to Ronny, but a moment later, as she feels her inability to repay Ronny for his help, she becomes sceptical of the value of 'personal relations'. Her experiences have compelled her to question all her general assumptions about the civilised world and to become aware of her own limitations. ' "All the things I thought I'd learnt are just a hindrance, they're not knowledge at all." ' It is only a momentary flash of self-knowledge however. In response to the shallow conventional behaviour around her, she slips back into making further harsh judgements of Fielding.

Mrs. Moore has also been changed as the result of her experience at the Marabar caves. When she receives Adela on her return with Ronny, she shows none of her former warmth and understanding, but is hard, irritable, and takes no interest in the victim. It is only when Adela mentions her echo that the old lady begins to take any notice. Her answers to Adela's naïve questions illustrate her greater capacity to accept the 'message of the caves', to hear a message that transcends human speech, to renounce the world of personal relations and endless questioning of fact and circumstance, and to find peace in rather cynical contemplative passivity. ' "I'll retire then into a cave of my own." ' Partly to avoid idealising Mrs. Moore and partly to prepare the reader for her departure and death, Forster presents her as cynical and apathetic.

'Why all this marriage? . . . The human race would have become a single person centuries ago if marriage was any use. And all this rubbish about love, love in a church, love in a cave, as if there is the least difference, and I held up from my business over such trifles!'

Mrs. Moore, apart from recognising the limitations of her Christian faith, has seen how relatively trivial is the social superstructure that Western civilisation has erected over the primitive instincts of man. Nevertheless the fact that she is shown as being deeply conscious that she has become a 'worse not a better woman' as the result of her experience in the cave, adds pyschological depth and complexity to her character and prevents her from assuming a purely symbolic role.

'A bad old woman, bad, bad, detestable. I used to be good with the children growing up, also I meet this young man in his mosque, I wanted him to be happy. Good, happy, small people. They do not exist, they were a dream. . . .'

The novel as a whole does not entirely endorse Mrs. Moore's pessimistic judgement. The desire for the happiness of another, in Aziz, Fielding, and Godbole, continues to be seen as the highest good, even if the desire is often frustrated. The author's control of perspective emphasises that good, small people do exist, even if they do not attain great happiness. For example, in the interview between Adela and Fielding after the trial, their stature may be diminished to that of dwarfs by an alien cosmos, but their human dignity remains untouched.

One of the most remarkable aspects of Chapter XXII is Adela's sudden recognition that she may have made a mistake. Although unsympathetic readers may complain that an alien 'spookiness' is allowed to enter the narrative here, as in the reference to the 'ghost' of a man run over by the Nawab Bahadur's car (based on an actual incident recorded in The Hill of Devi), a close reading of the text reveals how carefully Forster prepares us for Adela's moment of doubt. She has read the sentence about Aziz's innocence in Fielding's letter, Mrs. Moore acts as a touchstone of truth, there have been mentions of cave and echo, and as soon as Adela names her supposed attacker (everyone else has avoided referring to him by name), she escapes momentarily from her hallucinations. Her echo disappears. All this, of course, foreshadows what happens at the trial. On that occasion Mrs. Moore's good influence is transmitted through the repetition of her name and not through her actual presence. At this stage in the narrative, however, Ronny compels her to repress her doubts and allow the machinery of justice to grind on. In court Fielding's presence with 'an Indian child perched on his knee' (XXIV) has a very different effect.

The significance of the chapter (XXIII) that describes Mrs. Moore's departure from India has often been neglected by critics of this novel. In fact, it adds to our knowledge of Mrs. Moore's experience at the Marabar caves; and, through the author's commentary, suggests a modification of her nihilistic vision. Of course it is not necessary to think that the caves represent the same things to everyone; clearly they do not. They have presented Mrs. Moore with a vision of 'the horror of the universe and its littleness'.

As soon as she landed in India it seemed to her good, and when she saw the water flowing through the mosque-tank, or the Ganges, or the moon, caught in the shawl of night with all the other stars, it seemed a beautiful goal and an easy one. To be one with the universe!

The way of simple acceptance (which is analogous to the Hindu way), the pursuit of beauty and goodness, fail her when the Marabar strikes 'its gong'. What it suggests is the existence of ineradicable evil, what it offers is a vision of infinity that she can neither ignore nor respect. In effect the caves force Mrs. Moore to deny the existence of beauty and heroism (one thinks of Forster's account of Beethoven's Fifth Symphony in *Howards End*). It is therefore vital to see that her last sight of India invites her to reassess this denial:

> presently the boat sailed and thousands of coco-nut palms appeared all round the anchorage and climbed the hills to wave her farewell. 'So you thought an echo was India; you took the Marabar caves as final?' they laughed. 'What have we in common with them, or they with Asirgarh? Good-bye!'

She had seen 'the indestructible life of man and his changing faces, and the houses he has built for himself and God, and they appeared to her not in terms of her own trouble but as things to see'. If it were not for this coda, this radical reassessment of Mrs. Moore's experience by the author, Mrs. Moore would not serve so successfully in the novel as a life-enhancing influence after her death. Much of the dissatisfaction with Forster's handling of Mrs. Moore has arisen from a failure to give this part of the novel its proper emphasis and not from any real failure on Forster's part to fuse psychological and symbolic levels of meaning in her characterisation.

(iv) *The Trial*. 'I'm afraid I have made a mistake'

The trial is a very brilliantly conceived piece of tragi-comedy, British and Indians behaving with almost equal absurdity. At the beginning and end, the impassive figure of the man who works the fan, the punkah wallah, symbolises the indifference of India—perhaps of life itself—to the fates of individuals: 'he seemed apart from human destinies, a male fate, a winnower of souls'. This is one of the many devices used throughout the novel to suggest the essential littleness of man in the whole scale of being. But because the Indian figure possesses a kind of primitive grandeur, an heroic almost divine stature, he seems also to suggest a contrast between the simple enduring qualities of life and the transient social machinery imposed upon them. Most obviously he throws into sharp relief the pettiness of the legal and social squabbling in the court.

Forster has said that the main divisions of the novel correspond to the three seasons, 'the Cold Weather, the Hot Weather, and the Rains, which divide the Indian year'. The swift approach of the intense heat is vividly suggested through exact details ('fans hummed and spat'). In India, the author comments, it is impossible to invest the retreat of man from the cruel sun with the kind of heroism and beauty that have been enshrined in European myths about the retreat from the cold. Although the British officials struggle to keep the wheels of administration turning, their attempt to challenge the climate seems absurd. Nevertheless the plans for the trial go forward. And Adela, after her momentary doubts about Aziz's guilt, falls into line and abandons her intellectual and vaguely agnostic position and her momentary flash of self-knowledge, 'resuming her morning kneel to Christianity. There seemed no harm in it, it was the shortest and easiest cut to the unseen.' The allusion to the 'unseen' contrasts her apathetic surrender to religious conformity with her finer intuitions of the infinite. After she has compromised her integrity in this timid fashion, it is not surprising that her echo returns.

The British and Indians exhibit their characteristic weaknesses at the trial: the British their racial 'hubris', the Indians their pathetic irrelevance. But it is this irrelevance that elicits the frequent memories of the absent Mrs. Moore and therefore precipitates the crisis. Adela sees Fielding with the Indian boy on his lap, a symbolic detail that might have been more firmly stressed, and she is reinvigorated after the outburst of shouting in which Mrs. Moore's name is travestied into 'Esmiss Esmoor, a Hindu Goddess'. When she rises to her feet to give evidence, the parts of her experience and personality that had previously existed in fragments come together. She 'connects'. As a result she is able to return in imagination to the caves; for the first time she senses the full connection between her engagement and her conversation with Aziz. What the reader now realises is that her fastidious pride in her rationality and social decorum had previously prevented her from acknowledging that she had sought from an Indian, a relative stranger, information or reassurance about love and marriage that she would have hesitated to mention even to her fiancé. Subsequently she has projected her own feelings of guilt on the innocent Aziz. This is perhaps what we may infer from the state of her mind before she confesses that she has made a mistake.

There is a strong suggestion here, as in the description of the religious ceremonies at Mau, that the highest truth that can be achieved arises from a transfiguring act of the imagination. As Adela's mind flashes back to the original expedition to the Marabar caves, she experiences a kind of imaginative 'retake'; all the details that formerly seemed so dull now acquire new significance. In contrast to her earlier naïve expectations and her determination to find everything significant, there is now a calmer acceptance of the scene—'she was of it and not of it at the same time, and this double relation gave it indescribable splendour.' She confesses she has made a mistake; Aziz is declared innocent and is released. After the brief moment of truth, 'life returned to its complexities'. The punkah wallah 'unaware that anything unusual had occurred, . . . continued to pull the cord of his punkah, to gaze at the empty dais and the overturned special chairs, and rhythmically to agitate the clouds of descending dust.'

(c) AFTERMATH

(i) *Changed relations, Adela, Ronny, Fielding; 'dwarfs shaking hands'*

The declaration of Aziz's innocence sets in train new complications and satisfies nobody. In the midst of the turbulent, irrational celebrations, Adela, Fielding, and Aziz are swept along in directions not of their own choosing. After the momentary clarity of Adela's vision, we return to the muddle, misunderstanding, and tangled relations that have prevailed from the beginning, although now everything is felt more intensely. Adela's moment of truth amounts to a renunciation of her people, but simplifies nothing; nor does it for Fielding who had earlier thrown in his lot with the Indians. Now after the trial Adela, 'Without part in the universe she had created', was 'flung against Mr. Fielding'. Strong forces outside the characters themselves are at work. The irresistible pressure of the crowd is brilliantly suggested through the description of its movement and disquieting smells, its aura of debased sovereign power. The confusing effect of the trial on the relations of the characters is stressed. At first Adela greets Fielding as 'her enemy'. Angrily he asks her why she does not return to her 'own people'. In the background the released Aziz pleads piteously with Fielding not to desert him, a reminder of his sense of desertion when arrested at the railway station—'Cyril, Cyril, don't leave me.' The dialogue now brilliantly defines the new confusion in human attitudes, while the description of the Indian crowd and the misplaced attempts of the students to lavish the fruits of victory on Fielding and Adela create a physical impression of the forces that sweep the characters along. There is a characteristic blend of comedy and seriousness. When the crowd mistakes Adela for Mrs. Moore, it not only reminds us of the discrepancy between external fact and subjective feelings, but suggests that even amid such confusion something of Mrs. Moore's good influence remains.

Fielding is perfectly aware that his ride in the carriage with Adela will be interpreted as one further example of the way the English stick together. He knows too that they may be attacked suddenly by the crowd which is at the moment fêting them. In fact their instincts for revenge take another form. The mention of Nureddin's name sends the crowd to the hospital; only Dr. Panna Lal's adroit self-abasement saves the hospital from being attacked. The scene is important in two ways: it shows the force of the mass hysteria released in consequence of the arrest of Aziz, and it offers an interesting parallel to the custom of releasing prisoners as part of the Hindu religious festival at Mau. There is an ironic contrast between the inflamed political atmosphere surrounding Nureddin's release and the mood of divine forgiveness and reconciliation in the last chapters.

The sense that Adela has renounced her people and been implicitly disowned by them is reinforced in a number of ways. No one, with the exception of Fielding, makes arrangements for her accommodation, and his ill-judged kindness sows the seeds of further suspicion in Aziz and his fellow compatriots. She is physically adrift, at the mercy of others, anxious not to give further trouble, subconsciously drawn towards self-abasement in her choice of the lowly Dak bungalow as a temporary residence. It is cruelly ironic that her sacrifice at the trial should be rejected by the Indians into whose camp she has now been thrown. Yet they were right to reject her, suggests Forster, because though the sacrifice 'came from the heart, it did not include the heart'.

Nevertheless, for all their obvious imaginative and emotional limitations, Adela and Fielding attain a degree of self-knowledge that is proof of their integrity. In the first of two important interviews (XXVI), they attempt to piece together the scraps of evidence about what happened in the cave. Adela's account is more matter-of-fact than the vision she enjoyed in court. Speaking to a fellow rationalist, she minimises the mystery. Even so, her explanation contains details which strengthen the idea that her experience was partly due to repression of feelings of guilt. Neither Fielding nor Adela is sufficiently self-aware to see Adela's 'illness' as pyschological, but as Adela traces its stages from its inception at Fielding's tea-party (when she unconsciously let slip that she would not stay in India) to the 'hallucination' in the cave, the reader, who shares the superior knowledge of the author, may tentatively piece together a psychological pattern. One of the disturbing aspects of this first interview is the importation of the liberal 'heaven' into the conversation. The author appears to subscribe to the unsatisfactory faith that one may not believe in heaven, but may believe that honesty gets us there. Irony is not entirely absent, but it does not dissociate the author sufficiently from this revealing trait in Fielding's liberal humanist character.

In the second main interview (XXIX), which occurs after the news of Mrs. Moore's death and Ronny's visit to the college to break off the engagement, the author's voice, moving in and out of the dialogue, offers an imaginative vision that lies outside the limited consciousnesses of Adela and Fielding, and that therefore succeeds in firmly establishing the limits of their understanding. One passage of commentary is crucial:

> A friendliness, as of dwarfs shaking hands, was in the air. Both man and woman were at the height of their powers—sensible, honest, even subtle. They spoke the same language, and held the same opinions, and the variety of age and sex did not divide them. Yet they were dissatisfied. When they agreed, 'I want to go on living a bit,' or, 'I don't believe in God', the words were followed by a curious backwash as though the universe had displaced itself to fill up a tiny void, or as though they had seen their own gestures from an immense height—dwarfs talking, shaking hands and assuring each other that they stood on the same footing of insight. They did not think they were wrong, because as soon as honest people think they are wrong instability sets up. Not for them was an infinite goal behind the stars, and they never sought it. But wistfulness descended on them now, as on other occasions; the shadow of the shadow of a dream fell over their clear-cut interests, and objects never seen again seemed messages from another world.

Greater self-knowledge on the part of the characters than in the earlier scene (XXVI) is certainly implied. But even so it is only the author who can indicate the life that is denied them as a consequence of their decent honesty, sober integrity, and failure to develop the imaginative and emotional life. The image of running a finger along a polished wall, used by Adela a little earlier, serves to define the boundaries of their sensibilities in comparison with those of Mrs. Moore—and, by implication, of the author.

> Were there worlds beyond which they could never touch, or did all that is possible enter their consciousness? They could not tell. They only realized that their outlook was more or less similar, and found in this a satisfaction. Perhaps life is a mystery, not a muddle; they could not tell. Perhaps the hundred Indias which fuss and squabble so tiresomely are one, and the universe they mirror is one. They had not the apparatus for judging.

It comes as something of a shock to find the thoroughly sympathetic Fielding reduced to the same dwarf-like stature as Adela. But by recognising Fielding's limitations, Forster transcends the limits of his own liberal humanist faith. Only when Fielding acts as a convenient sensibility to record the perfect harmony between man and his works in the Mediterranean, does he regain something of his former stature. But once again it becomes impossible to dissociate Forster's from Fielding's vision. If the order and beauty of the Mediterranean are used to measure the muddle of India, it is no less true that the testing of Fielding in India has revealed not only his own inadequacy but that of Western civilisation. Forster himself explores modes of being not allowed for in Fielding's view of the world and thus transcends the limitations of the characters he has created. Although Forster's ambiguous attitude to the mystery of India may at times seem unsatisfactory, the frequent oscillations between finite and infinite perspectives prevent one from abstracting any over-simplified rationalistic picture of life from the novel.

(ii) *A question of compensation*

The reader experiences the same surprise as Fielding when Hamidullah first mentions the demand for compensation. The unworldliness of the Indians has not prepared us for this consequence of the trial. Fielding feels the injustice of the 'queer honest girl' losing her money so deeply that he attains a state of mind rare for him, known mainly to Aziz, Godbole, and Mrs. Moore. Adela 'advances into his consciousness'; momentarily he gives way to the irrational belief that 'we exist not in ourselves, but in terms of each other's minds', an experience that he had known only once before, after he had defended Aziz's innocence at the British Club. When the feast held to celebrate Aziz's triumph is over and the Indian and the Englishman are lying on a roof looking at the stars,

Fielding feels compelled to ask Aziz to withdraw his demands. His sympathetic and generous defence of Adela's action is in strong contrast to the Indian's unforgiving attitude and brutal sexual innuendos. Here, as so frequently in the novel, misunderstanding arises between men as the result of differences in attitude towards women. Eventually the memory of Mrs. Moore persuades Aziz to act generously and withdraw his claim. Nothing brings out quite so clearly the different attitudes of the two men towards reason and emotion as their conversation on the Nawab Bahadur's roof, unless it is the failure of Fielding and Adela to concoct a satisfactory letter of apology. In the first, Aziz protests indignantly that emotions are not a sack of potatoes to be weighed; in the second, we see that the failure springs from Adela's lack of real affection for Aziz or Indians generally. Adela's discovery is most important. She is forced to recognise that her chief defect is her inability to connect. She admits pathetically, 'I can do this right, and that right; but when the two are put together they come wrong.' Like Fielding, however, she is unable to exploit her acquired self-knowledge for the purposes of spiritual growth and inner harmony. What she lacks are strong feelings and a sympathetic imagination. These alone can produce wholeness.

4.   Temple

(i) *The Hindu festival at Mau*—'*the transfiguring promise*'

When an interviewer asked Forster what was the exact function of the description of the religious festival at Mau, he replied:

> It was architecturally necessary. I needed a lump, or a Hindu temple if you like—a mountain standing up. It is well placed; and it gathers up some strings. But there ought to be more after it. The lump sticks out a little too much.

On the other hand, it may be said that the impressionistic brevity is a necessary part of the ambiguity and indecisiveness of Forster's total vision. This last section is in the nature of a brief coda that offers a muted epiphany and a partial reconciliation of the major discords of the novel.

The opening sentence strikes quite a new note. 'Some hundreds of miles westward of the Marabar Hills, and two years later in time, Professor Narayan Godbole stands in the presence of God.' Clearly we have escaped in space and time from the Marabar Hills and all they symbolise and are promised an apotheosis, a rending of the veil, an imaginative transfiguration. However it would be out of key with the rest of the novel if muddle were not still to prevail. It is one of Forster's main themes that a religion or philosophy which claims to embrace all life must be able to accept the comic and the sublime, the muddle and the mystery. In this respect Hinduism and medieval Christianity are one.

Forster's 'Letters of 1921' published in *The Hill of Devi* (1953) describe the festival of Gokul Ashtami in the state of Dewas Senior. He incorporated into the novel many of the amusing incongruities that he had observed, such as the fact that the band played the waltz 'Nights of Gladness' during the religious festival; he retained, too, the strange combination of religious devotion and high-spirited humour, beauty and tawdriness, expectation and disappointment. What he omitted altogether were the facetious asides. By the time he came to write the novel, his imagination had succeeded in penetrating the essential spirit of the festival, and he no longer needed this typically English form of refuge from the indecorous and unknown.

Some critics of this novel have suggested that Forster finally presents the Hindu religion as the only one that can embrace the universe, but his ironic treatment of the ceremonies and of Godbole makes it clear that his attitude to all religions remains one of sceptical detachment. The deception practised in relation to the Rajah's death suggests a hollowness at the centre and links this episode to the recurrent theme of the preference for what is socially and aesthetically satisfying over what is true. What Forster offers in this scene at Mau are the imperfect attempts of all too fallible human beings to give objective form to an ideal vision of harmony. It is not necessary to be familiar with Indian religious beliefs and customs to respond as Forster wishes us to; anyone who is puzzled by the details may find it useful to consult some of the following: the fuller account of Krishna's birth in the *Bhagwad-Purana*, Forster's description in *The Hill of Devi*, G. L. Dickinson's *Appearances*, J. R. Ackerley's *Hindu Holiday*, V. A. Shahane's discussion in *E. M. Forster: A Reassessment*. Certainly it is useful to know that when Godbole sings

> 'Tukaram, Tukaram,
> Thou art my father and mother and everybody.'

he is praying not to God but to Tukaram, who is the greatest mystic saint of Maharashtra, an exponent of the Bhakti cult, which emphasises man's union with God through love.

If we recognise that the failure of each of the main characters arises from an inability to love—to put oneself in the position of God and love the other and to put oneself in the place of the other and say to God 'come, come, come', we shall see the organic relationship between Godbole's religious exaltation and the rest of the novel. With undeveloped hearts and impoverished imaginations, the English characters cannot 'connect'; they cannot bring together into a single act of consciousness the random intimations of the good. This Godbole does when he impels the image of Mrs. Moore and the wasp into his consciousness, and, imitating God, loves each equally. His experience is a mystical one, inextricably related to his particular form of worship, but the idea of love and imaginative transfiguration may be easily translated into Christian or humanist terms. The liberation from selfhood, the discovery of unity in the spirit, which Godbole achieves, is one that is open to all, and is more profitably spoken of in terms of consciousness than in terms of specific religious beliefs. The need to connect reason and emotion, the head and the heart (a typical nineteenth-century Romantic antithesis) is further stressed by the allusion to the shrines of Head and Heart built to commemorate the selfless act of a young Mohammedan saint who obeyed the command 'Free prisoners', but whose head was cut off by the police. Images of potential harmony proliferate in this last section of the novel.

(ii) *Towards harmony and reconciliation*

In 'Temple' there are three crucial intimations of perfect harmony and two abortive attempts at personal reconciliation. Under the first heading come Godbole's vision, Aziz's meeting with Ralph Moore, and the collision of the boats; under the second come the reunion of Aziz and Fielding by the toy mosque at Mau, a scene of brittle explanation and bitter recrimination, and the last ride together. Without loss of realism the figurative language expresses the symbolic importance of these scenes. For example, the collision of the boats, like the death of Gino's son in the overturned carriage at the end of *Where Angels Fear to Tread*, is one of those abrupt symbolic climaxes dear to Forster's heart. It is a device to bring into sudden focus and final reconciliation the antagonistic forces in the novel. The plunging of the characters into the waters of the tank at Mau suggests a form of spiritual baptism, a form of purification. The sources of misunderstanding (the letters of Ronny and Adela) are scattered on the waters. The rain here—and indeed throughout the last section of the book—suggests the release of the forces of imaginative love. However, Forster deliberately avoids any careful rounding off, stressing the lack of an emotional centre to the day's events and the difficulty of saying what precisely had happened.

The collision of the boats brings harmony where rational explanation has failed. If Aziz's suspicions that Fielding had married Adela for her money seem absurd and his excited protestations petty and ignoble, Fielding's faith in the power of rational argument is no less absurd. Where Godbole had learnt the wisdom of 'completeness, not reconstruction', Fielding remains imprisoned within his rational universe, 'wanting to argue and reconstruct'. Only some sudden external force, the collision of the boats, can temporarily break down his rational defences and allow natural feelings to flow freely. But Forster is too honest a novelist to fake a happy ending by suggesting that the reconciliation will last. Thus, although Fielding and Aziz are friends and can speak without restraint when they ride together, their characters and ways of life have changed too radically for them to be able to continue as close friends.

Although it has been much criticised and often misunderstood, the last paragraph of the novel epitomises the oscillations between affirmation and retraction, vision and anti-vision, that have characterised the novel.

> But the horses didn't want it—they swerved apart; the earth didn't want it, sending up rocks through which riders must pass single file; the temples, the tank, the jail, the palace, the birds, the carrion, the Guest House, that came into view as they issued from the gap and saw Mau beneath: they didn't want it, they said in their hundred voices, 'No, not yet,' and the sky said, 'No, not there.'

In recapitulating the main images of the book, the paragraph places the ultimate failure of the two men to achieve a lasting harmony here and now firmly within the context of the symbols that constitute the novel's imaginative structure. It is neither a pessimistic nor an optimistic ending, but holds in solution the tensions between man and man, and man and nature.

5. *What is its Meaning and Value?*

What makes *A Passage to India* so profoundly satisfying a novel to which one frequently returns is its perfect combination of symbolic suggestion, psychological insight, and social realism. Few twentieth-century novelists have succeeded so well in fusing these elements. Where other novelists have seen the future of the novel lying largely in the development of one of these modes at the expense of the others, for example, symbolic suggestion in William Golding, psychological study in James Joyce, Forster has worked along fairly traditional lines. He has acknowledged his debt to Jane Austen, from whom he learnt a skilful combination of comedy and seriousness, mastery of dialogue and, as he himself says, 'the possibilities of domestic humour. I was more ambitious than she was, of course; I tried to hitch it on to other things.' On to visionary symbolism, one might say, encouraged by the example of Melville and D. H. Lawrence. The French novelist Proust showed him how to look at character in 'the modern subconscious way'. On the whole his success arises less from innovation and experiment than from bringing to perfection an existing form. It follows therefore that the meaning of *A Passage to India* does not reside in its symbolism alone, powerful and resonant as that may be, nor in its insight into character, deep and subtle as that is, nor in its presentation of social issues, but in the vision that embraces all three. The beauty of its design controls and contains its saddest and most disturbing implications. The dialectical structure, which consists of positive affirmation (Mosque), negative retraction (Caves), muted re-affirmation (Temple), is reflected in every detail of the novel's imaginative organisation.

The human issues are of permanent interest. Forster explores two main types of human relations: those between man and woman and those between man and man. Although he is more successful with the latter. the breakdown in each illustrates how difficult it is for one person to communicate with another. The reasons for this are complex. In the case of Adela, Ronny and Fielding the main cause seems to be a lack of imaginative sympathy; all in some degree suffer from the Englishman's chief weakness, 'an undeveloped heart'. But neither Mrs. Moore nor Aziz share this fault, nor indeed does the simple-minded Ralph Moore.

Aziz and Mrs. Moore trust their emotional responses without rationalising them; it is this that brings them together and makes them fellow 'orientals'. But it is also the victory of heart over head that brings about Aziz's troubles; he is too headstrong and impulsive and too easily entertains ignoble suspicions about Fielding. If no single character succeeds in connecting reason and emotion in an enduring balance, Mrs. Moore, Aziz, Professor Godbole, and Fielding come nearest to achieving the ideal. The ideal of the good is much more widely distributed in this novel than in *Howards End* where it is unconvincingly focused on the one character, Margaret Schlegel. Each of the characters in *A Passage to India* fails in a different way and for different reasons. The final effect is not one of pessimism but of qualified optimism, since we witness a variety of approaches to truth, each having something in common with the other, each having a relative validity, none being complete. The reader is invited to make an imaginative synthesis. The moral and imaginative effect of the novel is to make us more sensitive to the importance of love and imagination in human affairs, to make us sceptical of putting our trust in any one religion or creed, and to believe in the unique power of beauty and personal relations.